Andrew Chong

Digital A   n

adj. involving or
relating to
the use of
computer
technology

n. the technique of filming
successive drawings
or positions of models
to create an illusion of
movement when the film
is shown as a sequence

ava |Academia
the environment of learning

An AVA Book
Published by AVA Publishing SA

Rue des Fontenailles 16
Case Postale
1000 Lausanne 6
Switzerland
Tel: +41 786 005 109
Email: enquiries@avabooks.ch

Distributed by
Thames & Hudson (ex-North America)
181a High Holborn
London WC1V 7QX
United Kingdom
Tel: +44 20 7845 5000
Fax: +44 20 7845 5055
Email: sales@thameshudson.co.uk
www.thamesandhudson.com

Distributed in the USA & Canada by
Watson-Guptill Publications
770 Broadway
New York, New York 10003
USA
Fax: +1 646 654 5487
Email: info@watsonguptill.com
www.watsonguptill.com

English Language Support Office
AVA Publishing (UK) Ltd.
Tel: +44 1903 204 455
Email: enquiries@avabooks.co.uk

ISBN 2-940373-56-6
ISBN 978-2-940373-56-7

10 9 8 7 6 5 4 3 2 1

Design by Tamasin Cole
www.tamasincole.co.uk

Production by
AVA Book Production Pte. Ltd., Singapore
Tel: +65 6334 8173
Fax: +65 6259 9830
Email: production@avabooks.com.sg

Cover image:
Pocoyo/Pocoyo™ © 2005 Zinkia Entertainment S.L.

▶

title
U2 Vertigo Tour

animator
Onedotzero Industries

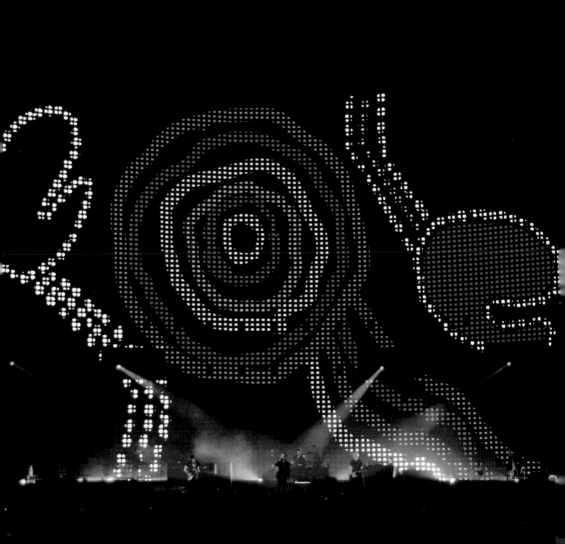

Contents

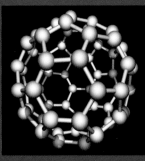

Introduction

Digital technology is the conduit for resurgence in animated features and animation in general. Technology's increasing power and spread into all areas of modern life give the opportunity for animation to be used in a wide range of technologies and contexts. Personal computers and digital media devices have made the medium more accessible than at any other time.

Marc Craste, Animation Director at Studio AKA, has suggested that: 'For a while, at least, the limitations of all but the very highest end computer graphics seemed to outweigh its potential. But for those of us not particularly interested in pursuing photorealism, or unable to even if we were interested, these limitations could sometimes work to our advantage.' Craste's remark is important for three reasons, which are fundamental to anyone seeking to engage with digital animation, theoretically or in practice:

▶ New technologies may often offer new opportunities for expression, but the animator or creator, not the software, must determine the nature of the work.

▶ Technical dexterity is not always required to be very creative with technology, which appears to offer an extraordinary range of choices, tools or applications.

▶ Embracing new technology and its potential does not mean abandoning previous core skills and knowledge. The old and new must always be brought together to achieve the most persuasive and original developments in the form.

The following pages will discuss how digitisation, new technologies and animation all combine to produce the end products which we know as digital animation.

Digitisation

Complex and heterogeneous media can be integrated because the foundation of most digital systems is binary. In simple terms binary, otherwise known as 'Base 2', is a counting method based on values that can only exist in two states: 1 or 0. Computers are programmed and operated using binary languages. Hence, for information to be handled by computers it must first be expressed or converted to a digital form.

In simpler terms, a computer is a machine that can count to 1.

For a computer to deal with data it must be translated into a form that can be measured in 1s and 0s. This process is termed digitisation.

Consider a light bulb. It has two states: on or off. This represents the smallest measure of information a system can hold: on or off, 0 or 1. This is known as 'bit'. A light bulb can be used as a 1-bit information store, and because it is obvious when the state is on or off, you could also say it has a simple visual display built in.

By increasing the number of light bulbs at your disposal, the amount of information you can store and display increases exponentially. With two lights you may achieve four states: both off, off and on, on and off, both on. This may be expressed thus: 00, 01, 10, 11. Hence, two lights allow you a 4-bit system.

Eight bits in set is called a byte. The byte is the basic packet of information that computers deal with.

The power and sophistication of the machines available to the untrained, non-technical user means that we never usually see anything in a binary form; the closest we get is when a device crashes and text warnings appear, or if we are adventurous enough to program a website and step into the world of HTML. These are examples of codes that let humans talk to computers.

It is important for the digital animator to have knowledge of the fundamentals of digital technology so as to better harness the potential of digital tools and media.

▶

title
The Painter

creator
**Hewlett-Packard
Development Company LP/
422 South**

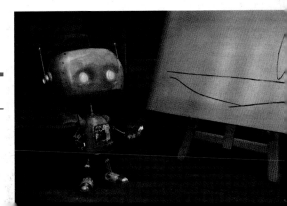

Animation

The basic principle of animation can be defined as a process that creates the illusion of movement to an audience by the presentation of sequential images in rapid succession.

An absolute definition of animation is not as straightforward as some texts may portray. On a practical basis, whether you work with pencils, clay, or pixels, the creation of movement is a form of magic – the techniques of which have been developed by the pioneers of film and are in a constant process of evolution and refinement by subsequent generations of animators.

The physiology of the human eye has evolved to facilitate a wide range of requirements. Human vision has its highest resolution in the centre of its field of vision. A concentration of the colour-detecting nerves (cone cells) means you see well what you are looking at directly. The less receptive expanse of the retina remains sensitive to movement, and even in environments of poor ambient light human sight is very sensitive to movement.

The development of visual illusion and moving images has held a particular fascination for audiences and film-makers alike. Even in our media-rich, image-saturated world, the first experiments in animation, such as flip books, still have the power to capture the maker and viewer alike.

Animation technique has some fundamental elements, which are unchanging despite the sophistication of the technology used to make it.

title
Machinima Island 2006

animators
Ricard Gras, Gareth Howell and Alex Lucas

Computers

Even before the computer first appeared, expectations and assumptions of such a machine's capabilities and design had existed. In the hundred years since Charles Babbage built his arithmetic calculating engine in 1822, moving pictures had developed from curios like the phenakistoscope and zoetrope into a global industry and new art form.

Through the portrayal of the imagined future worlds in films such as *Metropolis* (1927) by Fritz Lang and *Things to Come* (1936) by William Cameron Menzies, a global public were offered a vision of machines with visual displays that could store and deliver information and control mechanical processes.

The very aesthetic of electric or electromechanical devices – comprising keyboards, dials, switches, screens and the ability to perform multiple operations – was unlike anything that had come before. Fantasy and science fiction were responsible for the foundation of video and computer-based moving images.

In an era of ubiquitous digital technology it is difficult to imagine a time when computers were the stuff of dreams and science fiction. The iconic image of a screen with a keyboard and mouse atop a box with slots and lights is only applicable since the mid 1970s. The historical facts of computer technology are at odds with public perception.

The fundamentally screen-centric notion of computers conflicts with the truth that with few exceptions, computers were programmed and used with an interface based on rows of switches and lights requiring laborious and expert effort to perform any task. However, the portrayal of computer technology in cinema and popular fiction has always presented an image of computer technology with assets and capabilities beyond reality.

This predictive power of film proves a constant and recurring theme in the development of digital animation.

Despite an increasingly well-informed and media-literate audience, the actuality of creating digital animation is often misunderstood. By examining different and perhaps some less popularly celebrated examples, *Basics Animation: Digital Animation* will reveal some of the complexities and variations within digital animation production.

This book aims to demonstrate the relationship of core animation skills to the modern technologies, showing the similarities between the pioneers of animation and the evolution of computer-based practice. It will also show the continuing development of the language of animation.

▶

title
Things to Come

director
William Cameron Menzies

Digital animation

Foundations

This section studies the roots of digital animation. Early mechanical developments are explored and the first animated films are looked at in more detail. The chapter will also discuss the beginnings of modern computing.

Pioneers

This chapter explores the convergence of computing and cinema and how the two media influenced each other. It also looks at early animators and the techniques they used.

Development

The influence of computer development is discussed along with the initial key advancements in computer technology, which made the medium more accessible to the general public.

Maturity

Explores the ways in which digital animation has become available to media professionals, allowing for bigger projects without the necessity for budgets of a Hollywood, multinational or governmental scale.

Integration

Looks at how various media are used within one project and how digital animation allows for cross overs and cohesion.

Predictions

This section provides forecasts on future possibilities and projects as digital animation becomes more accessible to everyone.

How to get the most out of this book

This book serves as an introduction to digital animation – for those entering the field or working in related practices. The range of the content establishes the position of digital animation in the wider context of film-making and animation, including historical perspective and the development of the practice. Examples of current digital animation practice illustrate the diversity of those who use digital tools, and the constantly evolving nature of the technology.

Chapter openers introduce the key information to be discussed in each chapter.

Page numbers are located on the top right corner of each spread.

The impact of digital technology at the beginning of the twenty-first century has made the production and delivery of animation easier than ever before. A general adherence to Moore's Law means the tools available to animators are increasingly sophisticated and powerful, producing spectacular and extraordinary imagery. Concurrently, embedded technology and standardisation allow novice animators a simple path into the field. Digitisation has democratised the making of media; digital cameras, digital music and the Internet mean the tools of production are now available at a domestic level.

With the complexity of computer systems discreetly embedded behind simple graphic user interfaces and friendly control panels, digital animation can be an intuitive process that is accessible to the non-technical and even the non-animator. Digitisation in diverse fields also means diversification for animation – from flashing LEDs on a microwave oven to a surgical training simulator. Digital animation is not only reaching new peaks of achievement, but broadening in its application.

title
MirrorMask

director
Dave McKean

Integration

Chapter navigation highlights the current chapter unit and lists the previous and following sections.

Digital animation

Section headings
each section has a clear strapline to allow readers to quickly locate areas of interest.

Subheadings
elaborate on the principles discussed in the section headings and provide relevant and useful examples.

Images
various works in digital animation bring to life and support the main text.

The Internet and animation

82 | 83

Development in games

In 1991, Alex Seropian and Jason Jones founded Bungie Software Products Corporation while they were students at the University of Chicago. Publishing games primarily for the Apple Macintosh, they developed the **Marathon series**, a **first-person shooter (FPS)** considered to be ahead of its time by many of the games cognoscenti.

At the opposite end of the FPS spectrum are games that defined the genre in the 1990s. These effectively demonstrate the rapid evolution that can occur in the technology underlying games and their basic design as audiences' expectations change and develop.

Doom (1993) by id Software is recognised as an early success in the FPS genre and is representative of improved 3D technology. The premise of the game is unsophisticated in terms of plot and gameplay. The user plays (controls) a soldier who must fight through consecutive levels of demons and zombies, which have appeared following a failed science experiment.

The production of *Tomb Raider* (1996) at Core Design Ltd had a far greater level of design in terms of plot, character and general gameplay. Perhaps coming at a later stage in the timeline of games technology meant that cinematic values influenced the design of the location, central character and the supporting cast. A strong narrative plot requires problem-solving skills and strategy, as well as action. *Tomb Raider* has been likened to *Raiders of the Lost Ark* (1981) and edged the game world closer to film.

title
Tomb Raider

creator
Eidos Interactive Limited

An ability to depict larger and more complex environments with a wider range of movement on the part of the user led game production to mimic film practice in generating specialist disciplines of set design, cinematography and scriptwriting as well as greater consideration for the design of character movement.

Domestic production

For many years, production was confined to established studios, training establishments or university departments. In the contemporary era, however, production has become relatively cost-effective because hardware and software are available to facilitate work, and the World Wide Web is a bonafide exhibition context. Think of yourself in the first instance as 'a producer'. Consider what you actually need to make a piece of work, and consult established practitioners, facilitators and wholesalers to cost a production, and think of a process by which the piece might be made. This might be as little as the purchase of a laptop, software and a requisite site spend – but even these need greater consideration before the creative process can start.

Marathon series a benchmark for the FPS genre of games. It was a series that shared many aspects of film-making, with considerable attention to detail in the creation of environmental graphics, sound, effects and character design. It had a strong narrative structure and a realistic feel.

First-person shooter (FPS) a video game genre where the player interacts in a virtual environment with the point of view of the active character.

Maturity

Running glossary
provides the definitions of key terms highlighted within the main text.

Captions
provide the title and director, animator or creator of the images used to support the main text. Also impart more information on the work being discussed.

Thinking points
offer particular thoughts, ideas and discussion points about the principles discussed within the main text.

Introduction > How to get the most out of this book

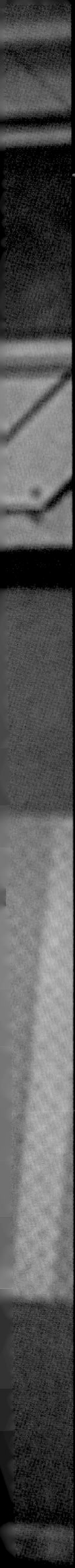

The roots of digital animation lie in the experimental work of the pioneers of cinema. The drive to make moving images at the end of the nineteenth century not only pushed the development of cinema technology, but is also a forerunner for the similar quest to utilise the computer for the same purpose decades later.

The origins of moving image technology are worthy of consideration to the modern animator as the mechanical crudity and limited scope of the resultant forms lay bare the fundamental building blocks of animation.

Animation has been a significant form throughout the history of cinema – prompting, informing and responding to each of the technological innovations in production. Animation can therefore be named as a modernist art – constantly developing an innovative language of expression related to other art forms, but equally, changing the phases of culture and society. Animation engages with and underpins 'modernity' in all its forms.

title
Metropolis

director
Fritz Lang

Animation shares its historical roots with cinema. The early experiments to make moving images used pictures created by hand. In the early- to mid-seventeenth century the process of photography required exposure times of hours, hence prohibiting its use to create image sequences for devices such as the zoetrope. The rapid refinement of precision engineering processes at the end of the nineteenth century and the adoption of standards to accommodate the industry allowed for developments in early moving images.

Various devices were revealed and superseded in the quest to perfect the discipline, with each innovation contributing to the next stage of development. For example, George Eastman's flexible photographic paper was used as recording stock by Etienne Marey in his moving picture camera, and this camera influenced Thomas Edison's development of the kinetoscope system.

The transition to flexible recording material – from paper to celluloid – allowed for an acceleration in technological development. By the turn of the twentieth century companies specialising in motion picture equipment and the production of films were established in the USA and Europe. The new form of cinema was developing its own language.

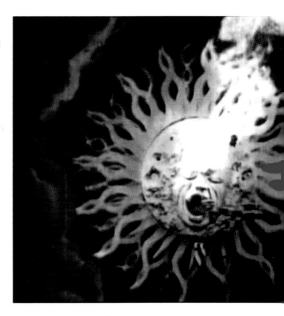

▲ ▶

title
Le Voyage à travers l'Impossible

director
Georges Mèliés

Use of flat artwork for props and sets are a direct transfer of Méliès's theatrical knowledge, but the use of colour and camera manipulation were the first techniques specifically attributable to moving images.

Trick films and the first special effects

In 1904, Georges Mèlié produced the fantasy film *Le Voyage à travers l'Impossible*, which employed many of the techniques developed during the production of his earlier **'trick films'**. The incorporation of illusory effects combined with live action is central to current feature-film special effects.

Mélié is often credited with being the originator of special effects. A pioneer film-maker, his contribution in the early days of cinema was to bring a sense of theatricality to the medium. Having performed as a magician, he used his knowledge of staging and narrative to produce what became known as 'trick films'.

Originally by accident and later by design, Mélié manipulated the camera to produce **optical illusions**. Examples of Mélié's techniques include stopping the camera and replacing actors or objects (the basis of stop-frame animation); under-cranking the camera so that action appears speeded up; and rewinding the camera and re-shooting on the same piece of film – an early form of optical compositing. Mélié even ventured into post-production, using hand-retouching techniques to physically colour the film.

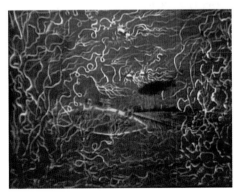

Trick films films produced by Georges Mélié using multiple exposures to give the illusion of people and objects metamorphosing or appearing and disappearing.

Optical illusion something that deceives the eye by appearing to be other than it is.

Early mechanical developments > The first animated films

Photography and sequential images

Eadweard Muybridge is claimed both by animation and cinema as the father of the forms – a legitimate claim in both cases, as the techniques and goals are still relevant in animation and cinema production. Even sophisticated computer-generated animation goes through a process of being realised as a series of still images before being assembled as a movie sequence.

In a quirk of history, Eadweard Muybridge carried out his original experiments in Palo Alto, California, where a century later many of the advances in computer imaging would be made. Commissioned by a stable owner to analyse the movement of a champion racehorse, Muybridge embarked on a five-year project to study and capture the horse's gait photographically.

The sequences of images that Eadweard Muybridge produced are often mistaken as frames taken from a movie. In actuality the images were produced using photographic cameras modified by Muybridge, using a custom-shutter system in order to achieve short exposures. This necessary adaptation was required to produce unblurred, individual images.

To create sequential images Muybridge arranged banks of his modified cameras perpendicular to the path of the horse and arranged cords to act as tripwires – triggering the camera as the subject passed.

Studying movement

Look carefully at Muybridge's sequential photographs and study at the dynamics of forward progressing motion. Develop simple line drawings that echo the horse's movement. These drawings may be the beginning of the development of more complex animation principles, but in the first instance, these lines might equally anticipate the joints and connecting principles of rigging in computer-generated animation. Drawn artwork used on the strips in a praxinoscope also closely resembles the way an animated sprite is assembled in **GIF** or **Flash** form. New processes are not so new.

Sequential artwork, cycles of movement, the relationship of timing and even the development of film language become clear by studying the evolution of moving image technology in its early forms.

▲

title
Scene still

photographer
Eadweard Muybridge

Often mistaken as images taken
from a movie film, Muybridge's
intention to analyse movement
not only provided reference
material for generations of
animators, but also exposed
the fundamental mechanics of
motion picture production years
before the technology had
been invented.

Early mechanical developments > The first animated films

Graphic interchange format (GIF) a system of compressing the information of a digital image
employing a restricted palette to reduce its file size.

Flash software released by Adobe in the mid 1990s as a vector-based animation and interactive
content package for the Internet.

The first animated films

In the early 1900s, as the technologies and techniques of cinema became more available and reliable, disciplines within the medium of film-making were already diversifying into specialist areas including animated film-making.

Animation, like other cinematic media, would be industrialised along the lines of factory-scale production, but the pioneering experiments of individual practitioners like Winsor McCay and Émile Cohl would continue. Meanwhile the medium that has its root in curiosity and fairground spectacle would become mass entertainment in the hands of Walt Disney and the Fleischer Studios.

Driven by the market and artistic endeavour, innovations in the production process, technological refinement and invention added to the palette of the animator; the medium developed from simplistic line drawings and manipulation of objects into the sophisticated imitations of life.

Celluloid (cel) transparent plastic made in sheets, formerly used for cinematographic film.

Foundations

Film and celluloid sheets (cels)

The process of assembling single images a frame at a time entered the cinematic realm in 1905 when Edwin S. Porter used a modified camera for his film *How Jones Lost His Roll* – the camera had the ability to advance frames in single increments. This would remain the basic method of animation for most of the twentieth century.

The use of celluloid or film impacted on the animation process in a further important way. Previously, the process of reproducing images was labour-intensive and difficult to control in terms of consistency. Animators exploited the translucency of paper in order to trace and develop sequences of drawings. Registration using the system of punched holes and pegs assisted with consistency and continuity, and was adopted by most animators in the burgeoning industry by 1914.

The use of transparent plastic made in sheets allowed not only for better consistency of line and image, but meant that production times could be shortened. Objects in a scene needed only to be drawn and painted once until they were required to move, and backgrounds could be single images over which the artwork of moving characters or objects could be laid.

title
Dream of a Rarebit Fiend

director
Edwin S. Porter

Many of the complex compositing techniques of current film-making practice can be seen in nascent form in the work of pioneers such as Edwin S. Porter. Miniatures, multiple exposure, matte paintings and replacement techniques are all used in *Dream of a Rarebit Fiend*.

Preparatory drawing

Paper and film cel remained the staple tools for drawn animation for several decades. With the advent of computers, such processes changed, making the 'in-betweener' or 'paint-and-trace' artist redundant. Despite the current use of computers in drawn animation, many animators and studios still produce original artwork on paper prior to digitising images. Animators often use drawing as a powerful exploratory device in developing imagery and constructing possible narratives, which are ultimately to be played out in CGI.

Animation can explain whatever the mind
of man can conceive. This facility makes it
the most versatile and explicit means of
communication yet devised for quick
mass appreciation.

Walt Disney

Foundations

Realism and naturalistic movement

title
Gulliver's Travels

animator
David Fleischer

Use of the rotoscope brought naturalistic human movement into the entirely hand-crafted and hand-animated space. In *Gulliver's Travels* the resulting action emphasised the fantastic nature of Lilliput and the traditionally animated Lilliputians.

Animation and cinema have a preoccupation with **realism**. This is not merely about making something realistic in a material sense, but creating authenticity, plausibility and the suspension of disbelief. The realism in any one narrative is not only concerned with the possibility of photorealistic representation, but also maintaining the terms and conditions of imaginary worlds that have been created.

Max Fleischer's 1915 invention – the **rotoscope** – was reminiscent of Leon Battista Alberti's 'Frame' from the fifteenth century. Technical developments such as these have always played a significant role in delivering realism in films. By projecting previously filmed action on frame one at a time and on to a screen, the movement could be traced to cel. The resulting movement is very naturalistic irrespective of the drawing method. This method was employed by the Fleischer brothers in their adaptation of *Gulliver's Travels* (1977).

Realism an artistic or literary movement or style characterised by the representation of people or things as they actually are.

Rotoscope the device invented by Max Fleischer, which allowed pre-filmed movement to be traced. Consisting of a projector that could be advanced one frame at a time, action could be displayed from below the frosted glass surface of a drawing board or animation disc, allowing the animator to use it as direct reference.

Early mechanical developments > The first animated films > The foundation of modern computing

Hyper-realism and planes of action

There are many similarities between the development of Disney's animated films in the period between *Snow White and the Seven Dwarfs* (1937) and *Bambi* (1941), and the Pixar Animation Studio between *Toy Story* (1995) and *Monsters Inc* (2001). Watch these films and see how both studios use their storytelling skills and deployment of technology to achieve ever greater degrees of realism – later dubbed 'hyper-realism' because of its self-evident artifice. The films become less like cartoons and more like live action.

title
**Snow White and
the Seven Dwarfs**

producer
Walt Disney

Disney's use of human movement for reference captures subtlety and elegance during scenes, such as the dance sequence and the above, and enhances the disquieting characteristics of the witch and mirror – a foreshadowing of what games and CGI animators call the Uncanny Valley.

Foundations

The Disney era

The advent of *Snow White and the Seven Dwarfs* in 1937 marked the beginning of what is widely regarded as Disney's domination of the medium. Although the Disney studio system adhered rigidly to its own conventions of character animation, it is significant that Oskar Fischinger's rotoscope technique was used for many of the sequences depicting the most human characters, namely Snow White and the Prince.

The use of 'real' human movement in animation through rotoscoping has often been contentious as the natural physically correct movement is recognisable when juxtaposed with classical and other forms of animation. Even when humans are used as subjects in the case of **pixilation**, the **stop-frame technique** creates an unnatural movement, which places the action in a particular theatrical context.

The friction between human movement and **key-framed** animation lives on in the use of motion capture. By recording human movement digitally and applying it to digital characters, it is possible to dispense with many of the laborious and expensive techniques of traditional animation. In successful uses of motion capture, the final animation is a blend of acting and animation.

Patented by Disney in 1937, the **multiplane rostrum** camera allowed the filming of several layers of still and animated artwork simultaneously. Each plane of artwork could be manipulated independently in three dimensions, which allowed a greater sense of depth and a method of developing a far more detailed environment. The use of planes in the digital era is commonplace and is an essential tool for animators, editors and effects designers. Planes are now also known as layers or tracks, and exist on an on-screen timeline rather than under a camera.

Pixilation a form of stop-frame animation that uses people and actors as puppets or props.

Stop-frame technique animation made by filming objects one frame at a time. Incremental changes of subject or camera between sequential shots resulting in an illusion of movement.

Key-frame the point of significant change in an animated sequence.

Multiplane rostrum a camera invented by the Disney Studios; it is mounted above several layers of artwork, which can be manipulated independently to enhance the illusion of three-dimensional space.

Early mechanical developments > The first animated films > The foundation of modern computing

▲

title
Kreise (Circles), 1933

animator
Oskar Fischinger

Using geometry and colour, Fischinger's brand of animation was closer to the art of painting than film.

Animation and modern art

There have always been a number of affiliations between animated film and modern art, mainly in the arena of experimental animation where many artists create exploratory non-linear, non-objective, abstract works. All animated films can exhibit modernist credentials, but such films show an ambition to create innovative, progressive, personal work, based on the interrogation of the formal principles of line, shape, form and colour. Most significantly, they demonstrate how they engage with the fine arts.

Abstract films

Animation outside of the commercial sphere would continue to be innovative and experimental. Despite having worked in commercial cinema during the Disney years, Oskar Fischinger produced animation of such an abstract and stylised nature that they could be mistaken for computer graphics.

The geometry and colour in Fischinger's animations were closer to the art of painting than film. Fischinger's work exemplified a leaning towards the fine arts rather than commercial cinema, which was far more apparent in Europe. Experimental pieces such as *Night on Bald Mountain* (1933) by Alexander Alexeieff employed a pin screen to create images, while *Hell Unlimited* (1936) by Norman McLaren demonstrated an early use of multiple media, which predates digital compositions by half a century. Both films were also created with artistic and political motivation.

Fischinger's painterly approach to animation was what attracted Disney to recruit him to create a sequence for *Fantasia* (1940), illustrating the Bach section. The same artistic temperament made it a fleeting association as Fischinger was unhappy to work within the constraints and ethos of the Disney system. His adherence to abstraction resulted in work comparable to futurist and **expressionist** paintings, and his belief that animation could be a visual equivalent to music predicted and resonated with the work of John Whitney Sr.

> What's most important in animation is the emotions and the ideas being portrayed.
> I'm a great believer of energy and emotion.
>
> Ralph Bakshi

Abstract relating to or denoting art that does not attempt to represent external reality, but rather seeks to achieve its effect using shapes, colours and textures.

Expressionist a style in which the artist seeks to express the inner world of emotion rather than external reality.

Early mechanical developments > **The first animated films** > The foundation of modern computing

The 1960s saw the arrival of a generation of machines that resembled what contemporary viewers may recognise as modern computers. With Alan Turing's model of multifunctional, programmable hardware adopted as standard, computers were no longer bespoke designs, but produced in numbers and sold to a range of end users, with specificity of purpose only occurring when the machine was programmed.

In the previous decade, a single computer would occupy a room, often having to be assembled on site and requiring the constant supervision of support staff to maintain it. A reduction in size following the replacement of vacuum valves with transistors – then followed by transistors with integrated circuits – led to a class of moveable, if not portable, mini computers: general purpose, affordable machines (in comparison to a mainframe), which could be operated by a single person.

The evolution from the transistor as the fundamental building block of electronic equipment was a major accelerating factor in the development of digital tools at the beginning of the 1960s. Pioneering research by Jack Kilby and Robert Noyce at the laboratories of Texas Instruments in the USA produced the first integrated circuit – a single component with the functionality of multiple transistors.

Integrated circuits

The integrated circuit (IC) solved several problems related to electronic engineering. The simplification of the component meant it could be fabricated more cheaply on an industrial scale. The use of fewer components also meant an increase in reliability in the component itself, hence the device or application in which it was used.

The miniaturisation of transistors within each IC added to the efficiency of the component as each switch required less energy to operate; this in turn allowed for larger, more complex assemblies and less energy consumption.

Developments such as the incorporation of a screen added to the computer's flexibility and provided the opportunity to experiment with graphic images for the first time. Examples of such developments are the first computer game – *Spacewar* – and the first graphic interface – Sketchpad. Sketchpad was a stylus-based screen controller devised by Ivan Sutherland in 1963.

Integrated circuit (IC) an electronic circuit formed on a small piece of semiconducting material, which performs the same function as a larger circuit made from discrete components.

▲

Colossus computer

courtesy of
The Art Archive

Colossus was the first analogue
programmable computer, which
helped the Allies to decipher
German encryption during
The Second World War.

Moore's Law

In 1965 Gordon Moore postulated an
observation on the relationship between
the unit cost of producing an integrated
circuit, the number of transistors in that
circuit and development over time, which
was published by *Electronics Magazine*.

Moore's observation was made by
empirical study of the computational
potential of early mechanical computers
from the 1930s to the point in 1965 when
he was working at Intel. This observation
was termed a law in later years by
Professor Carver Mead at the California
Institute of Technology. By extrapolation,
Moore predicted the doubling in number
of transistors in an integrated circuit every
eighteen months, until at least 1975. In
actuality, this prediction has held true for
three further decades and is expected to
do so until the 2020s.

The first animated films > The foundation of modern computing

The history of digital animation is formed by the convergence of cinema and computing. The relationship between the disciplines has formed the language and influenced the development of both. As with the evolution of film language and technology, computing has often been progressed by the invention of pioneering individuals and specific breakthroughs.

Historical documentation of the early days of moving pictures refers to the recognised pioneers and landmark technological developments that advanced the medium. Similarly, there are some familiar names at the beginning of digital animation, such as John Whitney Sr, Edwin Catmull and Douglas Trumbull, who all contributed to the initial adoption of computers in the film industry.

Also resonant with early cinema is the impact of individual developers and enthusiasts working with technology at consumer level. Bill Gates and Paul Allen's creation of the Microsoft Basic computer programming language for the Altair computer brought computers a step closer to the general public; Steve Wozniak's design of the Apple II delivered that promise and Andy Hertzfeld's graphic user interface opened the door for the rest of the world to use computer technology.

◀

title
2001: A Space Odyssey

director
Stanley Kubrick

At a time when computers were programmed using punch-cards and dials, and the results of their calculations delivered on vernier scales or illuminated valves, it was with considerable investment of time and effort that the earliest artists attempted to access computer technology to make moving images.

Like the pioneers of cinema technology, the early computer experimenters were mainly individuals motivated by personal interest to develop existing work with new tools. The spirit of exploration required considerable patience and investment owing to the limited accessibility of early computers to novice or untrained users.

Although much of the imagery then may seem crude or simplistic by modern standards, the achievements of the animators who made the first steps with computers is made more remarkable when one considers the unfriendliness of computer technology, which still used ticker tape as a standard output.

Early computer animation

John Whitney Sr was one of the first to use computers in order to create animation. His early work is indicative of the dissemination of technology and its appropriation for artistic use. Whitney's foundation in traditional animation, both commercial and experimental, enabled him to adapt the computerised targeting mechanism from an anti-aircraft gun in order to control the movement of a camera, producing geometric patterns of light and shade. He collaborated with Saul Bass, a graphic designer of repute, who began building a famous career for film title sequence design in the mid 1950s.

John Whitney Sr was able to pursue abstract animation with digital computers when he was made artist-in-residence at IBM in 1966. Recognised equally by arts institutions and commercial enterprises, his efforts and motivation are prophetic of the drive to use the technology for creative expression, and also to bring the form to public attention.

title
Vertigo film promotion

animator
John Whitney Sr

The films of geometry, light and colour produced by John Whitney Sr were some of the earliest computer animations made. The production method involved a significant amount of traditional photochemical processing – the initial output medium being monochrome film, which would be optically printed to create colour, multiple images and other effects.

In the animation world, people who understand pencils and paper usually aren't computer people, and the computer people usually aren't the artistic people, so they always stand on opposite sides of the line.

Don Bluth

◄

title
Animal Farm

animator
Halas & Batchelor Studio

John Halas and Joy Batchelor
were two of the first and most
influential British animators. Their
studio created the first full-length
British animated feature, *Animal
Farm* – an adaptation of George
Orwell's fable based on the
Russian Revolution.

Graphic design and motion graphics

In the contemporary era, it is possible to
encounter various design idioms –
sometimes in motion – alongside each
other, but graphic design as a discipline
was for many years an entirely separate
one from animation. John Whitney Sr and
Saul Bass anticipated the advent of
screen-based, motion graphics, which
combine traditional design concerns:
the use of type, aesthetic distinctiveness,
effective communicative signifiers and the
ability of forms to move and transform.
Moving graphic designs – dubbed 'motion
graphics' – have become the staple of
many commercials and independent
animation shorts.

Experimental animators > Early special effects

The 1960s was an era of divided public attitudes to all things scientific. At the height of Cold War anxiety President Kennedy had announced America's intention to put a man on the moon, while in Europe the Soviets erected the wall to divide Berlin. Depiction of computers reflected the range of sensibilities from optimism – in the case of the original television series of *Star Trek* (1966) – to the darkly satirical in *Dr Strangelove* (1964). With an increased understanding and awareness of computer technology through new, popular science journals and an increase in science fiction, the public perception of the computer and computer graphics were shaped by their presence in popular culture.

Science fiction's predicted image of screen-orientated computers in cinema and television did not reflect the state of the technology at the time. Jean-Luc Godard's *Alphaville* (1965) featured a real mainframe computer, which was a direct contrast to Stanley Kubrick's HAL 9000, in *2001: A Space Odyssey* (1968).

The reality for the animators tasked with creating the screen graphics for the simulated computer screens would have been using punch-card programs to operate their rostrum cameras and animation stands in order to achieve smooth movement. Yet the final images permanently shaped popular perception of computer imagery.

The illusion of space travel

Stanley Kubrick was one of the first directors to successfully deliver the illusion of space travel on the big screen. However, his vision of the future was at odds with the technology employed to produce it.

Kubrick's famous perfectionism and uncompromising directing style was matched by a screenplay founded on the technical expertise and scientific knowledge of Arthur C. Clarke (author of the original novel *2001: A Space Odyssey*). The successful illusion of space travel and exploration in *2001* was achieved through design based on Clarke's best predictions with reference to the NASA space program, combined with convincing visual effects by Douglas Trumbull.

The countless computer displays, video monitors and instrument panels were simulations created by film projectors hidden within each set. The text and graphics displayed on the screens were created by photographing physical artwork, which were then animated using mechanical techniques based around an Oxberry rostrum camera.

The environment presented, which was embedded with discreet technology, and the portrayal of a computer as the central character, were created with such convincing attention to detail that they impacted on the design aesthetic of not only subsequent science fiction films, but also the design of the technology they were simulating – from the physical objects to the graphic treatment of visual display units.

▲

title
2001: A Space Odyssey

director
Stanley Kubrick

In an era of public antipathy to science, Kubrick offered a convincing vision of the future in which screen-based technology and computers pervade all aspects of life using traditional film techniques and analogue computer technology.

Special effects

Animation was traditionally a 'hidden' special effect in live-action cinema, added in post-production; in the contemporary era it seems to be a major part of every feature film. A number of animation and new media critics have now suggested, therefore, that all cinema is animation, and not merely a subset of it.

Look carefully at a range of films and identify the following elements: explicit and obvious 'animation' (e.g. *The Hulk* (2003), flight scenes in *Spiderman* (2002)); possible animation made invisible by its context (e.g. crowd scenes in *Titanic* (1997)) and scenes which seem free of animation or other kinds of digital intervention (e.g. sequences without effects or manipulation, based on actors working in real locations).

Thinking in this way will enable viewers to deconstruct cinema in a spirit of talking about its meanings and effects, and also encourage investment in knowing about practical techniques and applications.

Experimental animators > Early special effects > The birth of computer games

The birth of computer games

Prior to the arrival of computer games in arcades and as consoles, computer technology was restricted to the work place and usually only operated by trained staff. Video games brought computer technology into the public domain and the home, and repositioned it as entertainment. Although rudimentary, the screen graphics also presented a real example of computer-generated imagery.

Games consoles established a route for computers to be used in the home. Since they utilised a television screen to display the actual video game, the subtle but important association was made between the familiar and benign technology of television. This was the first stage of the domestication of computer technology.

Arcade games and consoles changed the relationship between the public and computer technology by being embedded inside what was effectively a toy. The computer had introduced itself to a wider world, delivered the first training sessions in human-computer interaction, and established a new set of aesthetic values in the language of computer-generated imagery.

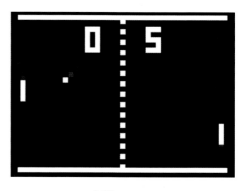

▲ ▼

Atari 2600

creator
Atari

Atari was one of the first video games consoles manufacturer, launching a console version of the video game *PONG*. Both *PONG* and Atari have been influential in the development of video and digital games.

The first video games

Despite limited graphic capacity and simplistic design, computer games were immediately popular when they appeared as consumer products. Early video game consoles and kiosks were the foundations for an industry that would expand on a global scale.

PONG represents year zero in the computer video games industry. It has been referred to as a simple tennis simulator, with its three interacting rectangles and a dotted line. *PONG*'s arrival as a coin-operated game in kiosk and tabletop form in 1972 was an instant success; within a year Atari launched a console version, which could be played at home through a television.

The simplicity of the game belies the impact of its arrival. Games arcades up to that point had comprised of pinball, air hockey and 'one-arm bandits'. To have control over the function of a digital device (even if only to move a block up or down) was not just novel, it was science fiction come true.

Games development had mostly taken place in the USA, but it was a Japanese game manufacturer, Taito, that would provide a breakthrough product, which included elements for a new genre of computer games. The launch of *Space Invaders* in 1978 had major repercussions in the nascent games industry – the elements of interactivity and the beginning of a narrative structure had been established.

Tomohiro Nishikado designed the game, assembled the hardware and wrote the code for *Space Invaders*, a title which, for a spell in the early 1980s, became synonymous with subsequent video games. A key feature of the gameplay was the computer-generated enemy. The interactivity was with a simulated opponent – one that had motivation and intent, and one that could return fire.

Novelty is only a small element of what *Space Invaders* offered. Games up to that point embodied a test of dexterity, electronic puzzles or a contest between players. *Space Invaders* pitted the player against a simulated enemy that had a single purpose: the invasion of Earth.
The objective of the game was to delay ranked alien forces from landing on earth by shooting them down with a sliding gun turret, simultaneously avoiding the enemy fire, which eroded the player's defensive barricades.

Early special effects > **The birth of computer games** > First CGI in cinema

Activity and interactivity

Games and gaming have prompted a
new form of spectatorship – one in which
the audience watches and participates
simultaneously. The concept of interactivity
in any form is predicated on the
relationship between understanding the
terms and conditions of participation,
and the technical dexterity to execute
intervention. Think about what is animated
and who is animating. How is action
motivated? How does narrative function in
a game? This will enable the game player
to think about how games are constructed
and how they relate to traditional forms of
animation and storytelling.

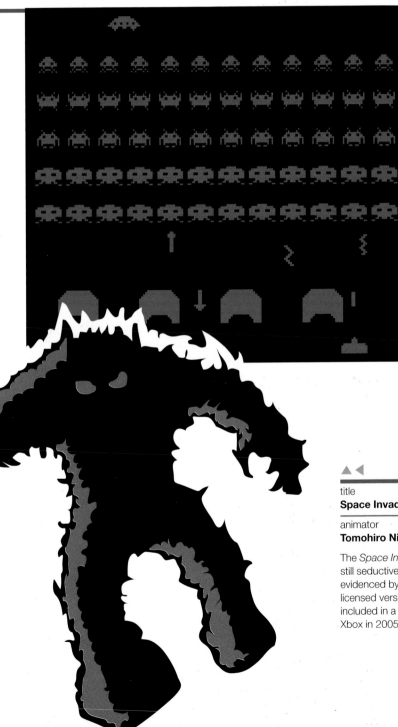

▲ ◄

title
Space Invaders

animator
Tomohiro Nishikado/Taito

The *Space Invaders* game is
still seductive and addictive,
evidenced by the fact that a
licensed version of it was
included in a release for
Xbox in 2005.

Early special effects > The birth of computer games > First CGI in cinema

The complexity involved in creating computer-generated images meant the expertise lay in the hands of engineers, scientists and researchers with only a handful of artists working with the direct intention of producing animation in an art and entertainment context. Until the arrival of establishments such as Industrial Light and Magic (ILM) or Pacific Data Images, any requirement of **CGI** for a feature film necessitated a relationship with an appropriate computer company or research laboratory.

Compared to what had been predicted by simulations of computer imagery, real CGI was limited in what it could provide for cinema. But for the early cases of digital animation in cinema the limited resolution was actually the required ingredient. The crude aesthetic was a genuine feature of CGI in the 1970s, and was a mark of authenticity.

The legacy of early computer graphics in feature films is a lingering audience perception of CGI as being primitive and plastic, with a community of CGI developers striving for ultimate realism to escape that public perception.

The playcentre for sensation seekers, where robot men and women do anything for you. And nothing can possibly go worng.

title
Westworld

director
Michael Crichton

The aesthetic of the computer-generated images in *Westworld* depicted the limited visual capacity of the technology portrayed in the film. Current audiences could easily interpret this prediction as an effect of encoding – a degredation produced by heavy compression of the video source, known to any cel phone videographer.

Computer-generated imagery (CGI) images that are originated within the digital environment.

Diegetic components of a film that exist in the narrative or created environment. For example, the sound of actors' voices are diegetic while a narrator's voice-over is non-diegetic.

CGI and diegesis

Computer-generated imagery was used diegetically for the first time in *Westworld* (1973). By processing individual frames of previously shot live action, John Whitney Jr, son of the pioneering animator, was able to replace the full image with a representation of a robot's point of view: that of a computerised compound eye. Although an effect rather than animation, the procedure is similar to the rotoscope invented by Max Fleischer for drawn animation.

Despite improvements in resolution, the use of digitally created animation required a context for inclusion in the plot. The crudity of imagery and mechanical motion meant that CGI was restricted to an effect rather than being an integral part of the live action. Feature film-makers still required the services of specialists recruited from universities and specialist technology companies to provide access to computer-generated imagery.

Futureworld (1976), the sequel to *Westworld*, saw the first use of three-dimensional computer-generated imagery in a feature film. The visualisation of 3D objects was beginning to produce imagery that was good enough to be considered for inclusion in more than the technical visualisation it had largely been developed for.

During the making of *Futureworld*, Ed Catmul, a computer science and physics graduate, designed an animated sequence depicting the construction of a robot facsimile for the central character played by Peter Fonda. Although primitive by current standards, the use of 3D CGI was a defining moment in film history.

▶

title
WarGames

director
John Badham

Rather than simulating computer video displays, personal computers became fast enough to deliver graphics and animation in real time, allowing directors to utilise actual computers in the diegesis. For *WarGames*, Apple II computers were used to provide graphics for the simulated NORAD computer.

Without any other points of reference, traditional portrayals of computer interfaces and screen graphics persisted throughout the 1970s with the reiteration of green wireframes and command line operation. Even with an increased presence of computer technology, the shorthand for computer screens was the predominant monochromatic, geometry-based visual displays. While the first real **graphic user interface (GUI)** would arrive in 1979, the schizophrenic appearance of computer interfaces alternated between the solidly traditional code-orientated screens to voice-controlled servants.

Public familiarity with technology was increasing and with it a new expectation of what computers should look like. The arrival of computer games, affordable domestic video recorders and the incorporation of liquid crystal displays (LCDs) and light emitting diodes (LEDs) into consumer electronics all made contributions to the visual vocabulary of actual technology, thus affecting how audiences received computer simulation and portrayal in film.

Alien

Despite the presence of a technologically enthusiastic visual effects supervisor in the guise of Douglas Trumbull, the deployment of CGI was restricted to the role of set design in Ridley Scott's seminal science fiction film *Alien* (1979). The reality of computer graphics at the time of the film's production meant Scott required the services of a computer software specialist to produce interfaces for the screens, computer terminals and flight controls on the film sets.

System Simulation in London was a software engineering company specialising in information systems and multimedia, creating information handling applications for mass data, text and image files. In order to create simulations and motion graphics for the film, System Simulation were required to write code in order to build software, which would result in graphic output.

Informed by the computer aesthetic of the time, various screens appeared in the film including a bank of flight controls echoed by command line interface and radar screens. Even a specialist computer company dealing with user interface design, having strong links to academic research into computers and art, did not have a graphic toolkit to make computer graphics then.

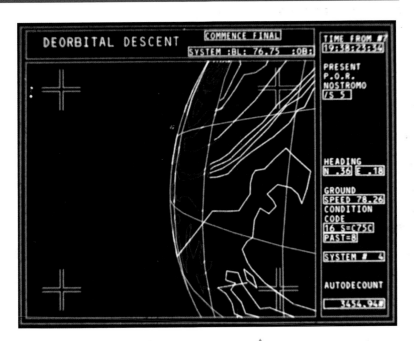

DEORBITAL DESCENT

COMMENCE FINAL
SYSTEM :BL: 76.75 :OB:

TIME FROM #7
19:38:23:34

PRESENT
P.O.R.
NOSTROMO
VS 5

HEADING
N .36 E .18

GROUND
SPEED 78.26
CONDITION
CODE
16 S=C75C
PAST=8

SYSTEM # 4

AUTODECOUNT

3454.948

title
Still from *Alien*

animator
**Flight control simulation
created by Brian Wyvil**

The influence of simulations
such as those in *Alien* can be
traced to the more sophisticated
graphic interfaces of modern
flight controls, vehicle satellite
navigators and applications,
such as Google Earth.

Graphic user interface (GUI) the system of interaction with technology based on images and icons
as opposed to text or code.

First CGI in cinema > GUIs and SIMs

Star Wars

By the mid 1970s computer imagery and animation had come to wider public awareness through science-fiction films, television and the arrival of the first home- and coin-operated video games. The limited palettes and crude graphics were not yet capable of producing imagery and animation for inclusion within the narrative of a live-action film or traditionally made animation without having the context of a technological framing, as was the case in *Westworld* and *Futureworld*.

A major impediment was that many computers, even the most advanced ones, were still based on an analogue foundation, with the final output limited to filming a video screen. But a precedent had been set by the quality of imagery in the public domain. Whereas previous depiction of computer displays in film had been pure speculation, the simulation of computer graphics within the diegesis would have to consider the audience's knowledge of actual CGI aesthetics.

Unlike the holographic Death Star and countdown monitor in *Star Wars: A New Hope* (1977), the many and varied computer readouts in the film were produced using traditional, optical methods of animation. Although the aesthetic rules of block graphics, wireframe and flat colour gave the impression of computer-generated imagery, actual artwork was created physically and filmed with Oxberry rostrum cameras.

The use of motion control and optical compositing had not been used in such an intensive way for a decade since Kubrick's benchmark feature *2001: A Space Odyssey*.

title
Star Wars: A New Hope

director
George Lucas

This film set new standards in special effects at all levels, but contained only one scene using digital animation. However, this was the beginning of a relationship between a visionary director and a new form of cinematic production, which would eventually revolutionise the industry.

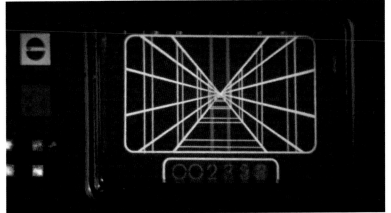

Blade Runner

In the film *Blade Runner* (1982), Ridley Scott depicted a computer interaction that would prove to influence not just the way people perceived computer technology. It defined an aesthetic for the portrayal of human-computer interaction, which has been copied consciously and unconsciously since computers have appeared in movies.

The famous scene in which the lead character, Deckard, uses an 'Esper' machine to forensically examine a 3D photograph also offered an aesthetic for future designers of real computer interfaces to aspire to.

The imagery in *Blade Runner*, although portrayed as ordinary and mundane, reinforced the futuristic nature of the film. Ironically, the images of wireframe vectors, such as those defining the navigation paths of Deckard's investigation, were produced using analogue techniques. They were actual drawings on cel, which were filmed on an animation rostrum before being played as movies through the various display units.

◀ ▲

title
Blade Runner

director
Ridley Scott

Although real-time navigational displays and the ability to scrutinise an image using computers are no longer restricted to the realm of science fiction, the experience and design of the interface of such tools comes not just from the functional developments of science and technology, but from their depiction in popular media.

Alternative digital histories

Inevitably, when thinking about animation history, it is often the case that work from the USA dominates analyses. It is important to remember that there is an alternative 'animation history' from nations all over the world. This is equally true in relation to digital animation – experiments in computer animation were taking place in Britain, for example, from the early 1970s. Make sure to find out about computer animation in other countries such as Canada, Japan, India, France etc as well. How have different artists in different cultures used available technology?

First CGI in cinema > GUIs and SIMs

Simulating computer imagery

In 1978, Douglas Adams's *The Hitchhiker's Guide to the Galaxy* was first aired on BBC Radio 4. Incongruous with, or perhaps due to, computer technology, Douglas's vision of a universe where computer technology was embedded into the fabric of the environment revealed a somewhat ambivalent and cynical view of technology.

In order to create the look and feel of a computerised book, computers had been considered to generate the imagery. However, the television adaptation of *The Hitchhiker's Guide to the Galaxy* required an immense amount of graphic design throughout the six half-hour episodes, so time and expense were prohibitive.

The alternative was to simulate a computer graphic aesthetic using traditional animation techniques. Rod Lord at Pearce Studios was commissioned to provide graphics for 'the Guide' and other screens on set. Physical artwork was filmed using a backlit technique with a rostrum camera to give the appearance of screen illumination. Movement was either created traditionally through drawn artwork or by using masks to reveal light out of dark. For appearances of the 'computer' animation on set, the action was back-projected on to screens, allowing the graphics to be recorded with the actors' performances.

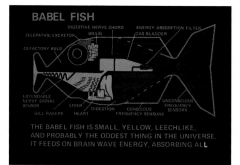

BABEL FISH

DIGESTIVE NERVE CHORD   ENERGY ABSORPTION FILTER
TELEPATHIC EXCRETOR   BRAIN   GAS BLADDER
OLFACTORY BULB

EXTENDABLE
NERVE SIGNAL
SENSOR   LIVER   UNCONSCIOUS
FREQUENCY
SENSORS
GILL RAKERS   HEART   DIGESTION   CONSCIOUS
FREQUENCY SENSORS

THE BABEL FISH IS SMALL, YELLOW, LEECHLIKE,
AND PROBABLY THE ODDEST THING IN THE UNIVERSE.
IT FEEDS ON BRAIN WAVE ENERGY, ABSORBING ALL

title
The Hitchhiker's Guide to the Galaxy *– for television*

animator
Rod Lord

The simulation of a computer style earned Rod Lord the BAFTA for best graphics in 1982. The images established a strong visual aesthetic, which influenced how following film-makers chose to simulate computer imagery.

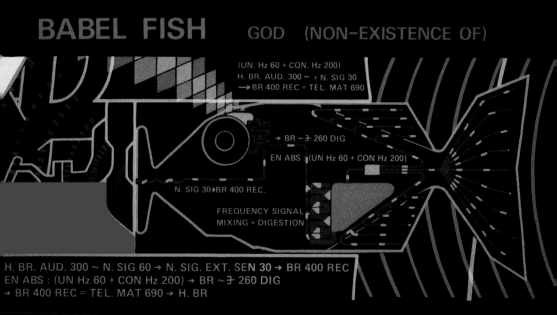

BABEL FISH   GOD   (NON-EXISTENCE OF)

(UN. Hz 60 + CON. Hz 200)
H. BR. AUD. 300 ~ + N. SIG 30
→ BR 400 REC = TEL. MAT 690

→ BR ~Ӡ 260 DIG

EN ABS : (UN Hz 60 + CON Hz 200)

N. SIG 30→BR 400 REC.

FREQUENCY SIGNAL
MIXING + DIGESTION

H. BR. AUD. 300 ~ N. SIG 60 → N. SIG. EXT. SEN 30 → BR 400 REC
EN ABS : (UN Hz 60 + CON Hz 200) → BR ~Ӡ 260 DIG
→ BR 400 REC = TEL. MAT 690 → H. BR

USEFUL COULD EVOLVE PURELY BY CHANCE, THAT
MANY THINKERS HAVE CHOSEN TO SEE IT AS A
FINAL AND CLINCHING PROOF OF THE
NON-EXISTENCE OF GOD.

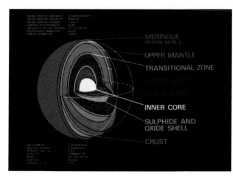

MERINGUE
OPTION 50 PL 3

UPPER MANTLE

TRANSITIONAL ZONE

INNER CORE

SULPHIDE AND
OXIDE SHELL

CRUST

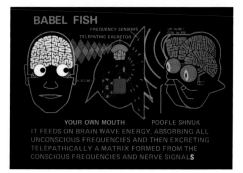

BABEL FISH

FREQUENCY SENSORS
TELEPATHIC EXCRETOR

YOUR OWN MOUTH   POOFLE SHNUK
IT FEEDS ON BRAIN WAVE ENERGY, ABSORBING ALL
UNCONSCIOUS FREQUENCIES AND THEN EXCRETING
TELEPATHICALLY A MATRIX FORMED FROM THE
CONSCIOUS FREQUENCIES AND NERVE SIGNALS

The earliest digital animation elements were restricted by budget, computer power and the technological expertise necessary to operate the few computers capable of image generation. As computers increased in speed, availability restrictions fell and the balance of power tilted towards the film-maker. The appearance of personal computers also gave hope for the rest of the general public.

As computers became established tools for image generation in engineering, architecture, mathematical modelling and related sciences, the graphic and animation capabilities improved and attracted more attention from the film-making community. Computing at the level required to 'deliver cinema quality imagery was only available to a few with budgets robust enough to access the machines and, importantly, technical support to translate the directors' ideas into images.

With computer technology reaching the masses on almost every level, as in the case of devices such as calculators and computer games, public awareness and interest in computers and computer imagery became first-hand and interactive. Upon the arrival of personal computers heralded by Apple's Macintosh and an icon-based interface that required little or no technical or computer training to operate, rudimentary computer-generated imagery became a possibility for individuals.

title
Dragon's Lair

animators
Rick Dyer and Don Bluth

Pioneers > **Development** > Maturity

Computer games development was prolific in the 1980s. Advancements increased the number of games titles being created and this segmented the industry into specific markets. Competition in arcades drove innovation in hardware and software, with game kiosks evolving into mock simulators and sit-on rides, while games graphics and animation became more sophisticated and eclectic.

Following the success of *PONG* and its clones, the variety and power of consoles increased with a clutch of manufacturers providing lightweight versions of the arcade titles, often translating the code for use on the burgeoning domestic computer market, with both technologies finding a place in the home as an addition to the television.

The low-power consumption of liquid crystal displays (**LCD**s) and light-emitting diodes (**LED**s) also allowed the games industry to develop portable, personal devices. They were limited in scope compared to their contemporary arcade and mains-powered cousins, but enthusiastically embraced by a young audience, which was predictive of the eventual ubiquity of personal electronic devices.

Interactive and accessible games technology introduced digital technology to a wider public in a non-threatening way, and increased the general awareness of computer-generated imagery and animation from the simplest LCD screen to fully resolved 3D simulators.

Vector games

While Nintendo began to miniaturise, Atari started to develop their vector-based games. Instead of shifting blocks of pixels around a screen, a vector-based approach used a microprocessor to calculate the changes of mathematically defined space, and displayed the resulting graphic using a wireframe representation.

The technique gave smoother animation and allowed for a far more variable range of movement in the 'gamespace'. Vector games generated a specific look and feel because they used the screen as an oscilloscope rather than a television screen.

Atari designer Ed Rotberg created a three-dimensional vector game called *Battlezone*. *Battlezone* was a forerunner of the 'first-person shooter' (FPS), which involved navigating a tank on a virtual battlefield while avoiding and destroying enemy tanks in order to score.

Such was the effectiveness of the virtual environment and interaction that the USA government commissioned a modified version of the game to be used as a training tool for drivers of Bradley fighting vehicles. Known as the *Bradley Trainer*, the vector game was a cost-effective alternative to simulators that were exclusively in the hands of bigger institutions such as Boeing and NASA.

▲

title
Donkey Kong

creator
Nintendo

The portability and playability
of the Game & Watch series
made them very popular – the
equivalent of iPods for the 1980s.

LCDs and LEDs

In 1980, Japanese electronic toy
manufacturer Nintendo launched a series of
hand-held electronic games under the brand
Game & Watch. The devices were ancestors
of the Game Boy and used the same
technology, LCD screens and circuitry as
digital clocks and watches. Graphics on
LCD and LED hand-helds were graphically
crude, low-performing devices. The graphic
elements were fixed in the display and
animation was achieved by illuminating or
switching between them. However, these
limitations did not affect the popularity
of the devices.

The Game & Watch series was popular
enough to last a full decade and generated
more than fifty titles, one of which was
Donkey Kong. It was so popular it was
developed into coin-operated kiosks and
table-based games and it was also
transferred to the burgeoning personal
computer market. Three versions of *Donkey
Kong* eventually appeared in the Game &
Watch series and the arcade versions were
rivalled in popularity only by *Pac-Man* from
the champion industry leader Atari. *Donkey
Kong*'s success transformed Nintendo into a
major force in the computer games industry.

Liquid crystal display (LCD) relies on a physical screen that can be switched between states to allow
or block the passage of light. The technology uses liquid filters with crystal structure or polarity, which
can be changed at a molecular level by the application of an electric current.

Light-emitting diode (LED) a semiconductor device that produces light when a current is passed in
the forward direction. The low-voltage elements produce a monochromatic light and are used in arrays
and matrices to form graphic displays.

Vector games part of the first generation of video games that used vector scopes for display rather
than TV-like, raster-based cathode ray tubes. *Asteroids* and *Battlezone* are the best known examples.

The first digital games > The animator's role

The animator's role

With the entry of digital imaging technology into film production and its use in the computer games arena, animators found opportunities to adapt traditional skills and expertise to help develop the implementation of new tools.

As with many innovations, digital animation was far from a singular discipline in its early incarnations. Achieving a particular look or effect often required a combination of techniques and technologies largely hidden in the final outcome.

This has often been the case in film-making. However, for those working in 'pure' computer graphics for interface design, games and simulation this was often new ground. In all cases there is always room for the application of traditional animation techniques to guide development.

The same requirement to depict movement with economy and expression had been developed and refined over time by cel, stop-frame and analogue animators and had been employed successfully in feature film production in the visual effects department. Early signs that traditional animation could have valuable impact in the digital realm are apparent in examples such as Disney's *Tron* (1982) and the computer game *Dragon's Lair* (1982).

title
Tron

director
Steven Lisberger

Recognised as a landmark film in computer animation, *Tron* relied on exhaustive control over the cinematography and optical compositing to allow coherence between the live-action elements and the computer-animated components.

I am an animator. I feel like I'm the manager of an animation cinema factory. I am not an executive. I'm rather like a foreman, like the boss of a team of craftsmen. That is the spirit of how I work.

Hayao Miyazaki

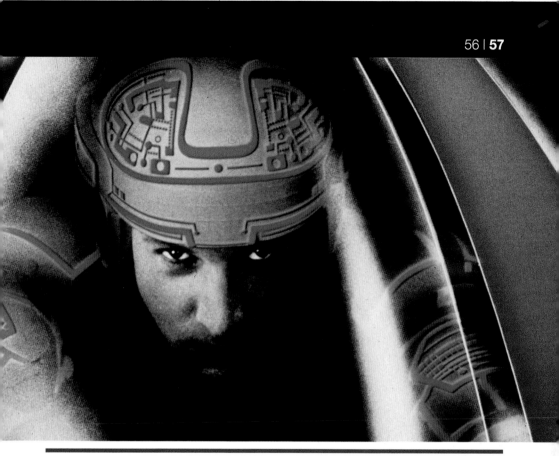

Digital imagery and film

Identified by many as the first significant use of digital animation in mainstream cinema, Steven Lisberger's *Tron* was groundbreaking beyond its unique visual style. The fact that it was a Disney film is remarkable in itself. A haven of tradition and famed for institutional convention, Disney's science fiction fantasy film took the brand in an entirely new direction from its staple output.

During this time, there was no in-house facility at Disney to create the digital animation sequences or computer effects seen in films such as *Tron*. An outside facility that could handle all animation and effects did not exist either. *Tron* employed an assembled team of CGI companies and experts from in and outside of the film industry. The film required not only the collaboration of animation companies, which worked with different and often bespoke systems, but combined cutting-edge digital image generation with techniques as old as film.

To achieve the glowing light effects in both live action and digital sequences the entire film was printed to cel and assembled physically under a backlit animation rostrum camera instead of using an optical printer. In practice, the entire film was assembled frame by frame like traditional drawn or stop-frame animation, although a large component of the artwork was created using computer programs.

It's the new golden
age of animation.

John Bloom

▲ ▶

title
Dragon's Lair

animators
Rick Dyer and Don Bluth

Bluth's fully-rendered animated
sequences set a new, high
standard and were the
ancestors of the 'cut scene':
miniature movies between the
playing levels in games.

Development

Animated and full-motion video sequences

Adventure games of the 1980s avoided the restrictions of relying on technology to produce imagery, but rather controlled the playback of pre-rendered media files from a library of video and sound. A good example of this is the game *Dragon's Lair*, which was designed by Rick Dyer. It was a concept that would predict technological advances and establish an approach to digital media.

The technological innovation of Laser Disc made it possible for *Dragon's Lair* to incorporate full-motion video sequences, a move which in turn required more expertise in the execution of the animation.

The fully-rendered animated sequences in *Dragon's Lair* were created by Don Bluth. Traditional skills and production values had never been seen before in a video game, and the quality of the Laser Disc format meant that image quality would not be reduced or compromised.

Unfortunately, the game had some inherent impediments. The focus of the gameplay on a player's ability to navigate a pre-determined path from animation to animation limited the scope for interactivity. As well, the innovative hardware made *Dragon's Lair* an expensive game to play. However, thanks to the cinematic animated sequences and strong design, the game was a success. This development blurred the line between games and films, and also treated players as audiences.

title
Dragon's Lair

animators
Rick Dyer and Don Bluth

Animation is about creating the illusion of life. And you can't create it if you don't have one.

Brad Bird

Game narratives

Animation plays an important role in telling stories – especially in the form of a game narrative.

There are essentially four game narrative models based on the degree of 'shift' between the gamer as narrator/author of the activity, and the narrative/challenge options set by the game itself:

Limited choices/challenges in a pre-determined linear narrative/goal.

Significant choices in a developmental narrative that affect the challenge/experience and the conclusion.

Extensive choices out of a range of sub-plots/activities/goals, which enable the creation of a principally gamer-authored experience.

Complete models of choice in which the gamer effectively builds the procedural narrative/challenge/experience.

Choose one of the above and try to develop a narrative that uses the principles of animation storytelling in the best ways to achieve an interesting gaming experience.

CGI aesthetics

The expense of producing high-quality digital animation meant that its early development resided in the domain of industry. Areas such as feature-film production, architectural visualisation and engineering could accommodate the cost of the hardware and expertise necessary to produce minutes or seconds of material.

This also shaped the aesthetic language of the animated form. The hard-edged quality and plasticity of models, combined with smooth camera moves, are not simply a result of the mathematical basis of computers. They are also derivations from the developments of imaging technology needed to satisfy markets, such as automotive engineering or environmental planning.

The aesthetic of CGI was also driven by early pressure to incorporate digitally produced images with traditionally filmed live action. This gap was beyond even the best facilities in the early 1980s. Subtleties of light, movement and both the organic or random nature of the real world contrasted and revealed the artifice of CGI. A struggle to attain photorealistic digital imagery persists in feature films to the present day.

title
The Last Starfighter

animators
John Whitney Jr, Gary Demos and **Ron Cobb**

The model and animation effects in the *The Last Starfighter* were entirely computer-generated.

Development

Computer-aided design (CAD) the use of computer technology for the industrial production of artefacts at the design stage in order to aid visualisation and planning.

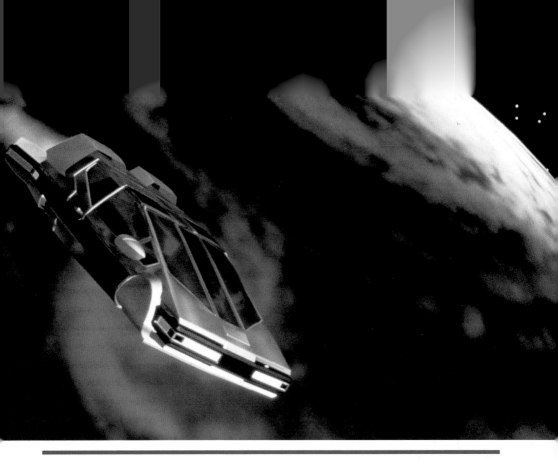

Computer-generated sequences

The Last Starfighter (1984) represents a benchmark in terms of the capability of digital imaging and animation. The model effects and animation effects in the film were generated entirely by computer, a feat requiring the use of what was at the time the most powerful computer available: the Cray Supercomputer.

John Whitney Jr and Gary Demos were responsible for providing technical expertise and creating the digital sequences, which required the highest level of realism yet seen in a feature film. The progress of computer technology and the development carried out by experimental animators, such as Whitney and Demos, brought digital animation closer to the mainstream.

Ron Cobb oversaw the production design of the film and bridged the gap between sophisticated computer technology and film-making. He worked previously with conventional materials and was an enthusiastic participant in the creation of digital imagery, having initial experience of CGI while designing the Nostromo flight consoles on *Alien*.

Cobb's understanding of traditional film practice and technique, coupled with a commitment to digital imaging, enabled him to design globally to achieve convincing transitions between live action and digital environments. Providing drawings for buildings, props and vehicles, it is notable that Cobb's design required a skilled **CAD (computer-aided design)** operator to translate the information into digital form.

Computer-assisted sequences

The Channel 4 and Chrysalis mini-feature, *Max Headroom*, shows the capabilities of digital animation tools during this point in history. CAD systems had been established in the fields of engineering and architecture, and had evolved from two-dimensional plan drafting tools into three-dimensional modellers used to visualise objects, buildings and environments at a planning stage.

Rod Lord used an engineering computer to animate sequences depicting a live computer display of a building in *Max Headroom*. The result was **computer-assisted animation** rather than computer generated. It was produced on a system that had been assembled to retro-fit new technology to established equipment. Unlike the Hollywood studios with feature-film budgets, animators at the broadcast level were pioneers of such processes – accumulating engineering, programming and electronics knowledge to attain the end result.

While **Paintbox** and **Abacus** were becoming more familiar facilities in graphics departments in the mid-1980s, digital character animation was still a distant goal, mainly due to the cost of equipment necessary for such an endeavour, but also because of the computational power needed to control complex, humanistic movement.

In spite of computer-generated imagery, the eponymous character of Max (who was supposed to be a simulated human in the film) proved to be beyond the capability and budget of the production. Max was created using make-up, latex, prosthetics, high-key lighting and editing to produce the trademark stutter and repetition. The high-contrast and vivid video colour emphasised the plasticity of the character, which mimicked the look of 3D computer modelling.

Computer-assisted animation the use of digital technology to enhance or manipulate recorded material.

Paintbox one of the original brands in digital imaging; a television and cinematic computer graphics tool created by Quantel for image manipulation and video effects.

Abacus an early digital frame store, often used to assemble composited or computer graphic sequences.

Development

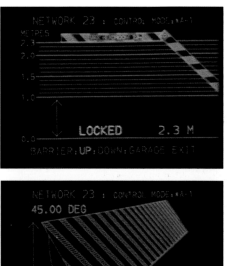

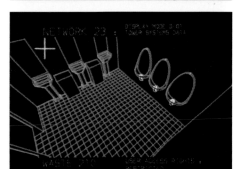

title
Max Headroom

animator
Rod Lord

Each frame of wireframe artwork in *Max Headroom* was displayed on a monochrome vector screen mounted in the bed of a rostrum camera then recorded on to film. Colours were achieved by placing gels over the vector scope – each colour in a frame requiring a new pass or exposure. The digital/analogue interface required a large component of human labour.

Character animation

The scope of what could be achieved by character animators working at the feature-film level was curtailed by the restrictions imposed by the governing commercial factors. In the 1980s, adding a digitally generated and animated character to traditionally filmed live action required compromise, control and the combination of multiple techniques and technologies.

Limitations on what could be generated in terms of subtlety of image, lighting and matching movement meant a persona could only appear by providing a context within the narrative to accommodate the look of the character. The lighting, camera movement and composition of the shot would have to be restricted to allow the addition of the digital elements. The entire production from the script through to post-production involved an awareness that digital animation would be part of the process.

Restrictions were less imposing in broadcast TV, specifically in music videos. MTV started in 1981 and offered a new audience for independent and experimental animators. Often in direct opposition to the dominant drive for photorealism and detailed modeling, the open form of the music video allowed animators to use less expensive technology to create short, character-based sequences within the context of a music video.

With fewer constraints and simpler tools, advancements made in digital animation started coming from broadcast studios and smaller post-production houses.

title
Gorillaz

animator
Jamie Hewlett

Music video characters have progressed to the point of featuring in live performances via plasma screens and later using angled reflectors, enabling the virtual band members to interact with live performers and the audience.

Music videos

The release of *Tron* influenced a generation of animators and film-makers to experiment with digital animation. While Hollywood pursued the goal of ever more photorealistic effects and animation, those in television and independent communities had to content themselves with more modest goals as the available equipment and expertise were far less powerful than what was available to film studios and effects houses.

At a time when digital animation and effects for television and video lasted for a few frames or seconds per sequence, the appearance of the first digitally animated music video at four and a half minutes stunned the video production community and offered audiences an alternate aesthetic for what was expected of computer graphic imagery. The music video 'Money For Nothing' was designed and created by Gavin Blair and Ian Pearson for Dire Straits, and featured a pair of caricatured workmen denouncing and envying musicians on MTV. Ironically, the video won MTV's best video award the following year.

Music video proved to be an ideal platform for experimental digital animation and provided an opportunity for animators to familiarise themselves with tools tolerant of original ideas and innovation.

More than a decade of technological development and music video became the subject for a prophetic William Gibson novel. Gibson's *Idoru* presented the idea of an entirely virtual rock star – a **hologram** – designed by a corporation visualised with holographic computer imaging and animated with artificial intelligence.

Appearing like a stepping stone toward that vision, the virtual band Gorillaz was formed by musician Damon Albarn and graphic artist Jamie Hewlett in 1998. The four-piece band of **avatars** is the public-facing expression of an indeterminate number of contributors and has only ever appeared in animated form, although the context of the animation has evolved throughout the band's history.

Reflecting the eclectic composition of the music, the Gorillaz visual world is an assembly of live action, photography, 3D computer imagery and 2D animation, which carries the strong graphic style from Hewlett's comic art. The digital mixture of sound is paralleled by the multifaceted animation.

Hologram a three-dimensional image formed by the interference of light beams from a laser or other coherent light source.

Avatar a movable icon representing a person in cyberspace or virtual reality graphics.

CGI aesthetics > **Character animation** > Computers for everyone

Digital characters

The early adopters of digital visualisation were in industrial fields, such as engineering and architecture. CAD systems had progressed to the point where technical drawings could be transferred to computer and digitised by manually re-plotting points from a physical print or blueprint using a puck and tablet. As CAD became embedded within the mainstream, further adaptations were made to integrate three-dimensional input for disciplines with a tradition of **maquette** and model-making in the prototype or visualisation stages of production.

Industrial Light and Magic (ILM) used a 3D digitiser in Barry Levinson's *Young Sherlock Holmes* (1985) to plot the coordinates of a maquette to build a 3D character of a stained glass knight – an exercise that required ILM technicians to write translation software in order to allow animators to use the captured data.

A distinguishing feature of effects and animation has been the necessity to fix the camera's position to allow for easier compositing, whether it is for physical effects, such as **matte paintings** and false front sets, or optical effects and post-production. The difficulty in matching action and change of perspective as a result of a moving camera meant this was avoided where possible. The knight sequence in *Young Sherlock Holmes* involves a camera track and dolly move, which starts in front of the character and revolves to follow him from behind. Rotoscoping was also at the core of the character's movement; filmed footage of an actor was done in profile and elevation to use as a key for the digital animation.

This development of Max Fleischer's rotoscope technique evolved into a fully digital form in the shape of motion capture. In 1985, the first CGI character required an actor's movement to be tracked by hand before being used to key frame a digital model. By 2001, the observation and recording of movement was fully digitised, while the work of tracking, recording and reapplying was all carried out by computers. The resulting distance between the actor and the digital character shortened considerably, helping with the delivery of digital characters as sophisticated as Gollum in *The Lord of the Rings* (2001).

Maquette a sculptor's small, preliminary model or sketch.

Industrial Light & Magic (ILM) George Lucas's assembled team of talented crafts people, originally founded in 1975 to help realise his vision for *Star Wars*.

Matte painting an image used to depict, enhance or modify the environment of a film sequence. Original matte paintings were physical objects placed in front of a camera and filmed live to obscure and replace an element of the frame. Modern versions may be digitally created and added live or in post-production.

Development

◀

title
The Lord of the Rings

director
Peter Jackson

The delivery of Gollum as a convincing main character requires the combined skills of several specialist disciplines. Texture, lighting, rigging, match move, compositors and an array of digital techniques contribute to the performance of actor Andy Serkis and the character animators.

◀

title
The Lawnmower Man

director
Brett Leonard

Hollywood's depiction of cyberspace gave Angel Studios the opportunity to test the boundaries between virtual and real worlds, creating digital characters with human aspects and simulated humans with digital characteristics. *Lawnmower Man* (1992) provides an insight into how practitioners at the cutting edge of computer graphics forecast the developing realms of virtual reality.

CGI aesthetics > Character animation > Computers for everyone

In order to utilise computers for animation, experimenters and pioneers were required to make a significant investment in educating themselves about digital technology – learning basic programming languages or understanding electronics. Even in feature-film production where dedicated effects facilities were using cutting-edge technologies, animators and cinematographers required partnerships with technicians and programmers to make effective use of the tools. For specialist services a relationship with research-and-development departments in industry or academic laboratories was still common.

The proliferation of electronics and a move on the part of a growing consumer market meant that computers were no longer the preserve of business. Early adopters of machines such as **PET**, **Spectrum** and **TRS-80** could now access the word-processing and accountancy tools, which had been the preserve of the office environment.

Innovation at the consumer level was less rapid in the early days. Storage of data was made possible by recording to audio cassette tape. Original machines lost their programming when the power was turned off. And these machines uniformly required the use of a command-line interface – a long way from how computers were being portrayed in film and television.

And then Macintosh arrived.

> Live-action writers will give you a structure, but who the hell is talking about structure? Animation is closer to jazz than some kind of classical stage structure.
>
> Ralph Bakshi

PET an early personal computer designed by Commodore aimed specifically at the small business user and domestic markets. The machine used a command-line interface and was equipped with a monochrome screen.

Spectrum launched by Sinclair in 1982, ZX Spectrum was one of the first colour-capable computers aimed at domestic users. Minimal in size and designed to work with televisions for visual display, the computer had mass appeal and was a favourite with early video gamers.

TRS-80 a consumer-level personal computer sold through RadioShack (Tandy in the UK) and was an early beneficiary of VisiCalc – a first generation spreadsheet application.

Development

◄

title
Original Macintosh icons

designer
Susan Kare

The design of graphic elements
for the Macintosh interface is
an exemplary exercise in the
use of a restricted palette and
indicative of the way in which the
computer-user demographic
shifted from the scientist and
technologist to the artisan
and generalist.

Apple Mac

From its inception, the Macintosh was
designed as a consumer-level machine.
Utilising the same functionality as its
predecessor, the Apple II, the Macintosh
used a graphical user interface (GUI) allowing
access to non-computer linguists and
setting the standard for personal computer
operating systems. The inclusion of a mouse
alongside the keyboard was also a first,
therefore allowing an even greater degree of
intuitive operation.

Apple Computer Inc had grown from
enthusiast and fan roots, when components
and information were just becoming
available outside specialist labs and
companies. The Macintosh maintained the
spirit and ideals of democratising the
computer as an open facility. From the
icon-driven controls of its user interface to
the ergonomic design of its case, the
Macintosh represented a leap towards
greater access to digital tools.

Designed from the ground up as an
affordable computer for the widest possible
application, it established the standard for
personal computer specification and was
symbolic of the widening availability of
digital technology.

Development and production of increasingly powerful computer imaging and animation equipment accelerated throughout the 1980s as new technology companies competed for a growing television market. The resulting imagery and animation grew more complex and ambitious, but the aesthetic was still largely mechanical and sterile as the producers of the work were either technically based or required to accommodate the code-based interfaces of animation-capable machines.

The distance between digital image-making and animation was maintained by the polarity of each discipline. Code writers and programmers were rarely film-makers and animators, and the expense of both practices meant experimentation was an expensive undertaking. Even when incorporated into television production, early CGI was a parallel rather than a collaborative facility. The resultant dominant aesthetic of CGI was lacking in many of the subtleties and sensibilities of established animation and film practice.

While designers struggled with operators' manuals and text-based interfaces, a breakthrough in digitally animated film would set a precedent for all to aim for. *Luxo Jr* introduced traditional animation techniques to a medium still developing its language.

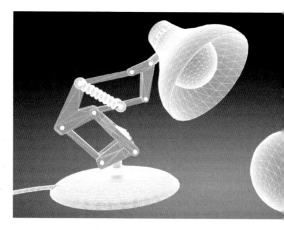

title
Luxo Jr

animator
John Lasseter

In a little over two minutes, *Luxo Jr* stunned a community of computer graphics developers. Designers were delirious to find out what plug-in or add-on Lasseter used to produce such an evocative and empathic film. The answer was simple: animation.

Organic movement motion denoting or characterised by a harmonious relationship between the elements of a whole.

Wireframe the basic visual representation of a digital object, in a digital version of a sketch. Boundary lines describe the volume of a virtual object.

Development

Traditional principles to digital form

When John Lasseter delivered his two-minute short, *Luxo Jr* (1986), a community of CGI artists was stunned by the animation. It was like nothing seen before in digital animation, and it caused a clamour to find out what the breakthrough technology was that could deliver such subtle and **organic movement** in characters. But there was no breakthrough technology, software or hardware. The animation in *Luxo Jr* may well have been unprecedented in the field of CGI, but it was familiar to any classically trained animator.

The pioneering step that *Luxo Jr* represents is the application of traditional animation principles to the digital form. Lasseter's unique position had allowed a close integration of the skills he learned as an animator at Disney with the technical expertise gained while at Industrial Light and Magic. The consequent animation in *Luxo Jr* was a hybrid of the best qualities from traditional practice and digital animation: naturalistic and expressive, combined with accurate mechanical representation and photorealism.

Luxo Jr stood against the dominant look of CGI in the 1980s, when audiences were used to flying logos, **wireframe** simulations and chrome in everything else. John Lasseter showed the CGI world a glimpse of the future of digital animation by employing the lessons of the past.

John Lasseter's 'secret components' to animation

Squash and stretch: Involves defining the rigidity and mass of an object by distorting its shape during an action.

Timing: The spacing of actions to define the weight and size of objects, and the personality of characters.

Anticipation: The preparation for an action.

Staging: The presentation of an idea so that it is unmistakably clear.

Follow through and overlapping action: The termination of an action and the establishment of its relationship to the next action.

Straight ahead action and pose-to-pose action: The two contrasting approaches to the creation of movement.

Slow in-and-out: The spacing of the in-between frames to achieve subtlety of timing and movement.

Arcs: The visual path of action for natural movement.

Exaggeration: Accentuating the essence of an idea via the design and the action.

Secondary action: The action of an object, which results from another action.

Appeal: Creating a design or an action that the audience enjoys watching.

The same difficulties faced by animators experimenting with computers were encountered by individual artists working with digital imaging tools – that of a technical barrier between the computer and the artist. Because many of the imaging machines were still command-line based, contemporary publications on computer art included a large component of mathematical theory and code – the central controlling elements for computers. For artists gravitating to the field of CGI, this inhibiting factor could only be overcome with a commitment to learning code or with the dedicated assistance of technical operators, who could act as translators of the artist's intent.

A similar barrier was faced by those moving in the other direction. Technically grounded individuals with aspirations to produce artwork using the computer were met with resistance or even hostility by a fine art culture that did not understand or accept the new medium. Despite having aesthetic elements from film, photography, sculpture, graphic arts, abstract painting and graphic design, the inability of critics and historians to comprehend the process or product of digital imaging established a barrier to animators and artists approaching the medium from a technical foundation.

title
Biogenesis still – Mutation X

animator
William Latham

William Latham helped bridge the wide gap between the artist and technology. He created forms, which he called 'computer sculptures'. By utilising software tools designed by programmers at IBM Winchester, Latham could affect the formation, transformation and deformation of objects in virtual space.

The best way for a beginner to write for animation is to closely watch animated films, then read the screenplays for them afterwards.

Douglas Wood

Development

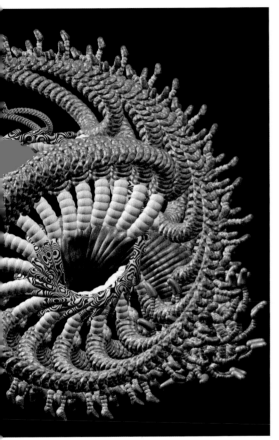

Computer-generated art

Fortunately for the practitioner, industry and science were more welcoming to the digital artist than the arts establishment. Understanding the value of diversity and inculcating thinking from outside established routes, companies and institutions such as IBM, MIT and Xerox encouraged artists with residencies, bursaries and technical assistance to experiment with computers and computer graphics.

Following in the footsteps of pioneers like John Whitney Sr, a new generation of artists were allowed to bring traditional skills and motivations to the field of computer-generated imagery through access schemes or direct commission.

In the UK, William Latham utilised the expertise of programmers based at IBM Winchester to create computer animations of complex geometric forms that evolve and reform into organic structures, which appear to have a biological foundation.

The precision and photorealism developed for engineering and simulation purposed in computer graphics can be utilised, developed and subverted when placed at the disposal of an artist with motivations that stem from painting, sculpture or even poetry. By combining the elements from both fields, the hybrid imagery produced reveals elements of each in a new light.

As the shape and structure of buildings have been radically influenced by the use of computers to plan and visualise the built environment, so computer-generated art has resulted in a new way of considering form as complexity and impossibility are rendered with convincing realism.

Photorealism

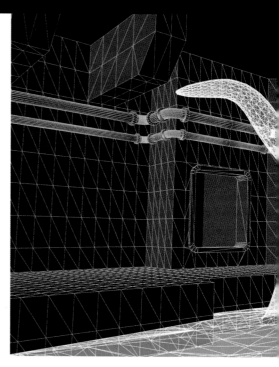

The end of the 1980s saw further development in the area of **photorealism** as computer graphics equipment offered incentives for software writers to improve specific areas of simulation and image creation. Cloth, fluid and lighting effects were high priorities as competition increased for a growing market at both broadcast and independent levels for digital animation and special effects.

Even with infinite resources there are limits on what computers can generate. It is rare that seemingly simple still images are produced only by a single tool. Modelling and rendering are separate issues even within the 3D environment, with embellishment often added with tools such as **Flame**, **Paintbox** or **Adobe Photoshop**.

When an animation project requires a photorealistic solution the animator must be aware of the diversity of techniques required to achieve it. What has helped the drive for photorealism is the digitisation of surrounding media, allowing the easy transfer of material between ancillary disciplines.

Photorealism the practice of creating artwork that is photographic in appearance. Photorealism is a dominant concern for simulation and invisible film effects where imagery is required to imitate real environments or match existing filmed material.

Flame a cinema and broadcast level digital tool used for compositing and visual effects creation.

Paintbox one of the original brands in digital imaging; a television and cinematic computer graphics tool created by Quantel for image manipulation and video effects.

Adobe Photoshop a suite of software tools developed as a mass-market accessible tool for photographic enhancement and retouching.

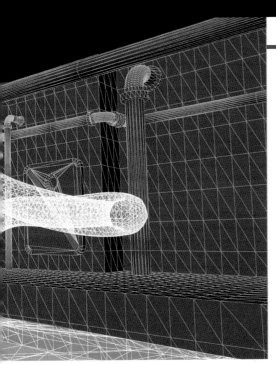

▲

title
The Abyss

director
James Cameron

The pseudopod sequence broke new ground in the merging of digital and actual film images, setting new standards in what audiences expected from cinematic special effects. The level of complexity and the convincing photorealism and physical simulation was also an effective promotional tool for the use of digital animation in mainstream cinema; it encouraged major studios to invest in their digital facilities.

Physical simulation

In Hollywood, the push to raise the bar higher was relentless. The brief for the 'water tentacle' sequence in James Cameron's *The Abyss* (1989) must have seemed a daunting prospect for the digital animators at ILM. The scene in which a serpentine column of water (pseudopod) grows out of the sea to explore a submersible station not only required an accurate depiction of flowing water, but also took place in real environments and interacted with live actors.

The complexities of rendering a realistic impression of water had been one of the holy grails for software developers. For the realisation of the pseudopod, ILM animators not only had to model the object virtually and convincingly distort the background of actual sets through its body – developers also had to consider the reflectivity of the environment on the water's surface, a surface that was constantly moving and rippling.

The pseudopod also had an acting role to perform: its 'head' moulded itself into the shape of the crew members' faces. Echoing the digital reproduction of Peter Fonda in *Futureworld*, film developers modelled the actors' faces using captured data. By capturing the various expressions of the actors, the crew could impose the forms on to the tip of the pseudopod and use a morphing transition to change between what were effectively key frames.

The 1990s was a period of stabilisation and fulfilment for many of the underlying technologies in digital animation and video production. Mainstream cinema and broadcast television were equipped with new tools designed specifically for non-technical designers and animators. The importance of digital animation was now accepted as a vital tool for visual effects departments, and the shift away from analogue tape to digital recording methods had begun in video studios.

Computer graphics became an accepted and expected component of video production at industrial levels, with even modest corporate productions featuring digital graphics and animation.

With equipment becoming more affordable, colleges and academic institutions developed media courses to meet the needs of the growing industry. Fine artists also discovered the computer's ability to manipulate and adapt traditionally crafted material or produce work in a virtual space.

At a domestic level, technology began to inhabit all areas of modern life. The public relationship with computers and computer technology changed with the arrival of the World Wide Web and personal computers. Games technology had given the public a first taste of interactivity with digital technology. PCs and access to the Internet allowed the home user to communicate on a global basis and use the technology available to create rather than simply consume.

title
Tomb Raider

creator
Eidos Interactive Limited

The Internet and animation

As technology is constantly developed and improved at the industrial level, the consequent benefits become apparent to the domestic user as previous breakthroughs become available to the public. The World Wide Web and computer games are important examples of how general users and the masses benefit from the rapid innovation of technology.

The hardware within games consoles during the 1990s could be traced to the flight simulator technology developed by commercial aircraft builders and military trainers. The familiarity with personal computers, Internet access through the Web and the performance of increasingly powerful games technologies raised the public's expectations of CGI. The masses could now access essential tools and this laid the foundations for domestic creators and publishers of animation.

The invention of a common language and protocols for a global network provided a new medium that was not simply for broadcasting – it allowed for response and interactivity. Furthermore, it gave impetus to the transition from analogue to digital in other media as the Web's ability to transfer text and images grew to include sound and video.

The World Wide Web

For many animators the Web has proved to be the missing piece of the puzzle: exhibition. From amateur to professional, the goal for any animator is to present their finished work to an audience – something that had previously been limited and restrictive.

The animation festival circuit offers an avenue for amateurs and independent labels to display their work. However, exhibition possibilities are limited as festivals are often only held annually at widely dispersed venues, hence catering for an elite or limited audience. For the professionals, work must often be tailored to the requirements of a broadcasting or distribution company's rules, and more often than not this avenue is not always the most liberal or tolerant of experimental and innovative work.

Web-based exhibition provides a far-reaching, alternative route to a global audience – as bandwidth increases and codes become more efficient, there is less compromise over the quality of the final piece. For both commercial and non-commercial animation, a generation of Web users and consumers is a viable first choice for displaying work.

You know that's part of the magic of animation, you can morph from one thing to another, it's something. I particularly abhor these animated films that just tell something which could have been done in live action.

Gerald Scarfe

▲ ▶

title
**How it was that
we got to be Angels**

animator
Gareth Howell

For current independent
animators the Web can be a first
choice for exhibiting work,
therefore avoiding the expenses
of distribution, touring and the
restrictions of institutional
censorship and control.

The Internet and animation > Digital animation in cinema

Development in games

In 1991, Alex Seropian and Jason Jones founded Bungie Software Products Corporation while they were students at the University of Chicago. Publishing games primarily for the Apple Macintosh, they developed the **Marathon series**, a **first-person shooter (FPS)** considered to be ahead of its time by many of the games cognoscenti.

At the opposite end of the FPS spectrum are games that defined the genre in the 1990s. These effectively demonstrate the rapid evolution that can occur in the technology underlying games and their basic design as audiences' expectations change and develop.

Doom (1993) by id Software is recognised as an early success in the FPS genre and is representative of improved 3D technology. The premise of the game is unsophisticated in terms of plot and gameplay. The user plays (controls) a soldier who must fight through consecutive levels of demons and zombies, which have appeared following a failed science experiment.

The production of *Tomb Raider* (1996) at Core Design Ltd had a far greater level of design in terms of plot, character and general gameplay. Perhaps coming at a later stage in the timeline of games technology meant that cinematic values influenced the design of the location, central character and the supporting cast. A strong narrative plot requires problem-solving skills and strategy, as well as action. *Tomb Raider* has been likened to *Raiders of the Lost Ark* (1981) and edged the game world closer to film.

Marathon series a benchmark for the FPS genre of games. It was a series that shared many aspects of film-making, with considerable attention to detail in the creation of environmental graphics, sound, effects and character design. It had a strong narrative structure and a realistic feel.

First-person shooter (FPS) a video game genre where the player interacts in a virtual environment with the point of view of the active character.

Maturity

title
Tomb Raider

creator
Eidos Interactive Limited

An ability to depict larger and
more complex environments
with a wider range of movement
on the part of the user led
game production to mimic film
practice in generating specialist
disciplines of set design,
cinematography and
scriptwriting as well as greater
consideration for the design
of character movement.

Domestic production

For many years, production was
confined to established studios, training
establishments or university departments.
In the contemporary era, however,
production has become relatively cost-
effective because hardware and software
are available to facilitate work, and the
World Wide Web is a bonafide exhibition
context. Think of yourself in the first
instance as 'a producer'. Consider what
you actually need to make a piece of work,
and consult established practitioners,
facilitators and wholesalers to cost a
production, and think of a process by
which the piece might be made. This
might be as little as the purchase of a
laptop, software and a requisite site
space – but even these need proper
consideration before the creative process
can start.

The Internet and animation > Digital animation in cinema

Digital animation in cinema

The demands within feature-film production drove the development of digital imaging and animation technology. Due to the high quality threshold for projected images, cinematic production is becoming a demanding environment for computer-generated imagery – requiring bespoke solutions for specific films or sequences.

With the increased use of CGI in Hollywood and digital animation becoming more common on broadcast television, film directors pushed for more challenging results from visual effects departments. A new culture of incorporation developed as the expectations of audiences grew and producers accepted and trusted the capability of digital facilities.

The culture of film production began to shift towards the digital in film production as the computer established its place in the mix of cinema technology. Other areas of production adjusted to accommodate the facility, for example, safety lines or flying rigs used to secure actors and objects during stunts, had formerly been camouflaged during the shoot. As computers would be used to remove the unwanted wires in post-production, wires could be highlighted during filming to make the process easier for the operator or even allow for automated removal by software.

Rendering

Exemplary of the increasing impact of digital animation technology in cinema is the 1993 award for Scientific and Engineering Achievement given by the Academy of Motion Picture Arts to Pixar's **RenderMan**. The software helped *Jurassic Park* (1993) gain the Oscar for Best Visual Effects in the same year. In 2001, the RenderMan team were awarded a full Oscar themselves.

Rendering is the final stage in producing three-dimensional digital artwork. Although further adjustment and **compositing** may be applied, the render stage of the 3D process translates objects and movement designed by the modeller and animator into the completed simulation.

Once models have been built, rigged and animated, the rendering software applies colour, tone, texture, lighting and blur to complete the image. The process is applied to stylised, as well as photorealistic, imagery. The recognition of the importance of the software signified the appreciation of how digital tools had now found their place in feature-film and animation production.

Since its first use in the mid 1980s, RenderMan had been an important tool in the creation of digital animation in films as varied as *The Abyss* (1989), *Beauty and the Beast* (1991) and *Death Becomes Her* (1992).

RenderMan a rendering application developed by Pixar used for digital effects and to integrate synthetic effects with live-action footage.

Rendering the part of digital animation associated with producing the finished image. Rendering adds aspects of lighting, texture and effects such as fluidity and atmosphere.

Compositing the addition or combination of several elements of imagery in the same sequence of film or video.

Maturity

▲

title
Beauty and the Beast

director
Gary Trousdale

Although famous for the traditional approach to animated features, Disney Studios has also been the site of invention and adoption of new technologies. *Beauty and the Beast* was one of the first major productions to use Pixar's RenderMan software to complete its digital sequences.

Technological advancements in cinema

Indicative of the changing attitude of studios to digital animation is the approach by directors to make CGI material central to the narrative. When James Cameron embarked on *Terminator 2: Judgment Day* (1991) the requirement for a digitally animated metallic robot – which could fluidly metamorphose into human form – was a challenge beyond anything previously achieved in computer graphics. The sequences that were eventually created by ILM required the facility to expand its CGI department and invest in $35 million worth of imaging technology.

The spectacular results were a landmark in cinematic CGI and won the Oscar in 1992 for Best Visual Effects. It also helped reinforce the place of CGI and digital animation in the industry, providing a benchmark for producers to allocate budgets for visual effects.

While the prominent sequences in live action features were obvious examples of digital animation entering the mainstream, the discreet use of computers to facilitate or enhance traditional production also increased. In collaboration with John Lasseter at Pixar, Disney had created a digital factory system to replace laborious tasks and enhance the compositing process – this is known as the Computer Animation Production System (CAPS). In CAPS, a suite of digital tools replaced many of the traditional roles. Rather than physical trace and paint, pencil animation on paper was scanned so that lines could be 'inked' digitally. Colour was then applied to the file rather than painted on a cel.

title
Beauty and the Beast

director
Gary Trousdale

Following the tradition of exploiting the best technological advancements, Disney's use of digital animation tools offered a new cinematic freedom to its animated features. The finesse of Disney's character animation was augmented by the computer's ability to animate geometric forms, with camera motion adding complexity and richness to backgrounds and environments.

Maturity

Disney's use of digital technology also found expression on screen when computers were used to create a camera move in *Beauty and the Beast* (1991) – the first use of digital animation in a Disney feature. The sweeping camera move with a constantly shifting perspective during the ballroom sequence was a composition of traditionally drawn elements for the dancing characters with digitally animated scenery, including a chandelier. This produced a final sequence that would have proved exhaustive, perhaps impossible, using traditional drawn techniques.

The combination of digital tools with traditional animation techniques produces sequences unattainable through purely conventional methods. Disney's innovation is now standard practice in mainstream animation. Television series such as *Futurama* and *Clone Wars* include traditional animation with digitally produced environments and props. Feature animations also combine the digital and traditional tools of production. *Belleville Rendez-Vous* (2003), for example, employs 3D CGI for geometric models and mechanical animation with some extremely exaggerated drawn characters in a traditional style.

Access and achievement

Although achievements in major cinema and television productions guide the way in showing the development of digital animation, it is clear that as technology becomes available in the high street or through college courses, students and practitioners start to create more improvised and localised experiments using new technologies. This creates a sustained output from student contexts and the beginnings of careers in the industry and as independent film-makers.

The Internet and animation > Digital animation in cinema > Digital animation in television

New tools

The appearance of new software was
pivotal in making the creation of digitally
animated forms accessible to the masses.
Video Toaster was a suite of hardware and
software tools that provided Digital Video
Effects (DVE), 3D-modelling, animation
and, in subsequent versions, non-linear
editing tools at broadcast standard for a
fraction of the cost of specialist, individual
solutions. The versatile solution was
quickly adopted by broadcasters and
production companies. However, it was
also affordable enough for corporate,
educational and hobbyist use, bringing a
set of digital animation tools within the
grasp of independent animators and
film-makers for the first time.

Adobe Photoshop was developed as
a mass-market accessible tool for
photographic enhancement and
retouching. It was produced as an
affordable tool for photography
enthusiasts and graphic designers.
The application was used to correct
minor glitches and artefacts remaining
at the end of a multimillion-dollar
production line.

Maturity

title
Spirited Away

director
Hayao Miyazaki

In *Spirited Away* (2001),
Hayao Miyazaki included
digitally rendered backgrounds
and props with traditionally
drawn character animation,
demonstrating an acceptance
of digital tools in current
production.

Digital animation in television

While Hollywood celebrated the achievements of digital animation in the cutting edge, high-budget feature films, demands on television production for comparable results were unattainable until the arrival of affordable graphics-capable personal computers.

A growing market at the broadcast level helped increase the number of developers working across the industry and directed output toward less-technical, budget-conscious television studios and colleges. An increased availability in affordable technology allowed many artists and designers access to digital tools for the first time.

Developments such as the **Video Toaster** suite were used to facilitate the effects and animation for television series such as *SeaQuest DSV* (1993) and *Babylon 5* (1993).

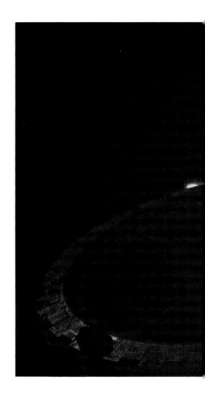

Even in hand-drawn animation, humans are widely considered to be the most difficult to execute, because everybody has a feeling for how they move.

Brad Bird

Video Toaster a suite of hardware and software tools providing digital video effects, 3D-modelling and animation.

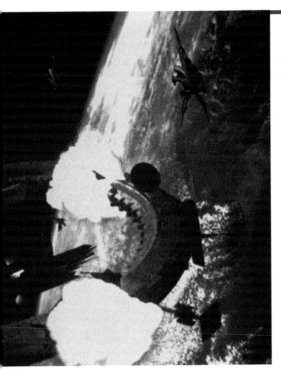

▲

title
Babylon 5

director
J Michael Straczynski

As personal computers delivered better video and graphic quality, visual effects in broadcast television began to approach the levels only seen in cinematic features. Video Toaster raised the bar in terms of audience expectation and is symbolic of the rise in personal computer power.

Special effects in a television series

J Michael Straczynski undertook a bold and ambitious move when he created *Babylon 5* – a futuristic science fiction series. With audiences now familiar with the effects work in feature films such as the original *Star Wars* trilogy and the first two *Terminator* films, expectations of work within the genre were high. When Paramount revived the *Star Trek* television franchise in 1983, the effects were created by the only people with the capacity to do so: feature film special effects companies, with a budget to match.

Usually requiring the same level of production and composition as cinema, special effects sequences for a television series were formerly designed to be as economical and versatile as possible. For example, generic ships could be recycled and composited with different backgrounds for subsequent episodes.

Babylon 5 was written as a continuous narrative saga rather than an episodic chain of stories requiring linear development. The arrival of Video Toaster allowed for CGI to become more integral in the narrative because once the digital cast of models and environments had been made, they could be re-rendered and animated in-house to satisfy new scripts.

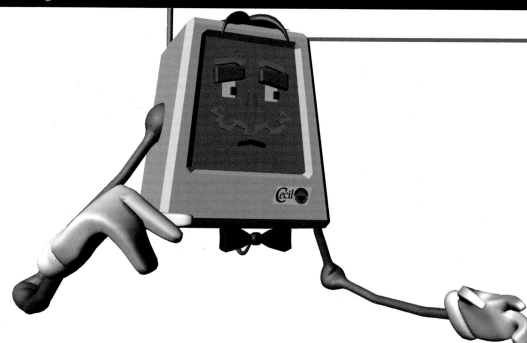

▲ ◀ ▶

title
ReBoot

creators
**Gavin Blair, John Grace,
Phil Mitchell, Ian Pearson**

Turning a limited palette to their
advantage, the creators of
ReBoot adapted visual elements
of game graphics to create an
alternate digital universe. The
world of Mainframe shows
striking similarities to current
Web-based virtual reality
spaces.

Maturity

Computer-animated children's series

Ian Pearson and Gavin Blair sowed the seed for a fully computer-animated children's series. Joining forces with scriptwriter John Grace and computer animator Phil Mitchell, they formed 'The Hub', which took nearly a decade to launch as the world's first computer-animated series. On its first airing in 1994, *ReBoot* was realised with some of the best CGI technology available.

In *ReBoot*, the environment of 'Mainframe' was originally conceived to accommodate the limitations of computer-generated animation. The use of the computer metaphor was not merely an accommodation for graphic restriction. By adopting the language and logic of technology, *ReBoot* space was sophisticated enough to break the genre and category for which it had been commissioned; it appealed to a far wider audience through layers of meaning and reference.

At the time of its final episode in 2001, *ReBoot* had reached an aesthetic closer to current computer games as opposed to pre-rendered cinematic CGI. However, the entire canon from 1994 onwards competes with, and often surpasses, current offerings created on technology that allows higher resolution and sophistication of final output. The core values that sustain the appeal and attraction of *ReBoot* are the same as those for all films, animated or otherwise. Script, acting, design, characterisation, music and all the elements that contribute to an effective film are central to every episode of *ReBoot*.

Because good writing in a TV cartoon is so rare, I think the animation on *The Simpsons* is often overlooked.

Matt Groening

Digital animation in cinema > Digital animation in television > Traditional skills in CGI

An inhibiting factor in the progress of digital animation in feature films was the language barrier. Projected images have to be rendered with such detail that the only computers available for this purpose required a dedicated technical operator to follow the director's instructions. Since technical operators are not always literate in terms of animation or film-making there is a danger that the original intent is lost in translation.

A significant change in the quality of animation and visual effects is apparent when the animators' skills are employed and successfully transferred to the digital realm. As technology improved and industrial practice matured, the roles of animators and technologists merged and they combined forces. By including animators in the development process as well as in production, the tools and execution benefited from the experience of experts with traditional skills.

With a greater understanding of the requirements for animation, software developers began to build applications that were sympathetic to the needs of industrial practitioners. Terms such as 'key frame' and 'easing' became part of the software interface; the timeline became a digital dope sheet and editing software adopted traditional cutting terminology.

First CGI animated feature

Such is the heritage of The Walt Disney Company that the word 'animation' is synonymous with the brand. To generations brought up on classic Disney titles, the image most associated with the term animation was that of Mickey Mouse. The appearance of *Toy Story* (1995) signalled a change in the cultural dominance of that association.

Toy Story was the first of a series of productions that would be made in a collaborative agreement between Pixar and Disney. The first entirely digitally animated feature film was the first of a scheduled five. The film was made with the fastest and latest digital tools and traditional animation principles.

The choice of subject – toys – accommodated the aesthetic capabilities of the available computer graphics technology. Setting the action in a virtual space also limited the realism of the human characters. However, it is the realisation of the central characters that makes *Toy Story* successful: Buzz and Woody are fully formed individuals. By following the conventions of traditional animation, the medium becomes transparent.

Toy Story is the result of John Lasseter's vision, unique skill set and fortunate synchronicity. With first-hand experience in the best-known traditional animation studio, as well as the leading special effects facility, Lasseter can be credited with driving the evolution of mainstream animation and renewing interest in the medium as a whole.

title
Toy Story

director
John Lasseter

Despite setting a high technical standard, the strength of *Toy Story* lies in the fact that all traditional elements were maintained: screenplay, acting, design and everything that requires attention in conventional film and animation production.

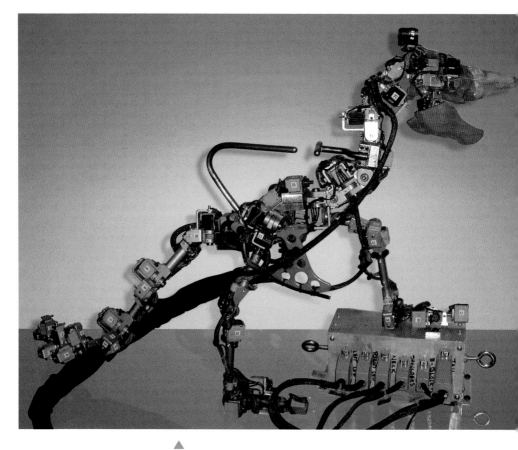

▲

title
Dinosaur Input Device

photographed by
Rudy Rucker

The DID is a physical icon of
the transition from analogue
to digital animation technology
for special effects. It is also
evidence of the relevance of
traditional skills for providing
the movement in either form,
independent of the
technology employed.

Maturity

Dinosaur Input Device (DID)

The adaptation of Michael Crichton's novel *Jurassic Park* called for close interaction with a variety of prehistoric creatures on a scale never attempted before in film. The creation of photorealistic dinosaurs for the film *Jurassic Park* (1993) exemplifies the impact and speed of evolution (sorry) of digital technology in a single production.

The original team assembled to supply the dinosaur animation brought skills covering a range of techniques both conventional and contemporary. Phil Tippett would provide the main performance of the dinosaurs through stop-frame animation, while digital techniques were being utilised in pre-production in the form of low-resolution storyboards and action blocking. In production, large scale animatronics for live action scenes were to be used for close-up details in interactions between actors and dinosaurs, and in post-production ILM would provide long shots of herding plains dinosaurs, plus digital enhancement of the stop-frame animation.

In a turnaround from its original plan, the animated sequences were to be realised digitally rather than through conventional stop-frame techniques, negating the need for digital processing of stop-frame images or interpolation. The ILM computer team scanned the physical models produced for animatronic work in order to generate the skin of the dinosaurs, while the Tippett studio fashioned a large-scale armature that incorporated sensors to generate data to be used by the digital animators. Named the Dinosaur Input Device (DID), the device was mounted on a motion control jib so the larger movements could be programmed into the most expensive flying rig in stop-frame history.

I had to catch up with where creative technologies had gone since I worked on the show, did some bohemian painting, and continued research into animation, studying the masters, developing new methods, styles, character studies etc.

Joe Murray

Digital animation in television > Traditional skills in CGI > Digital worlds and digital actors

title
Jurassic Park

director
Steven Spielberg

The combination of scientific research, expertise, skills and innovation resulted in the most convincing portrayal of prehistoric creatures ever seen and afforded the film major awards, including the Oscar and BAFTA for Best Visual Effects.

Maturity

Digital worlds and digital actors

By the end of the century digital animation technology had been adopted in animation and special effects studios as standard industry tools; thinking of digital solutions for cinematic challenges was now part of mainstream cinema production.

A generation of film-makers, comfortable and enthusiastic about digital techniques, would demand more of the effects and animation departments to realise visions previously impossible through conventional means – from the depiction of multifaceted worlds and seamless manipulation of time in *The Matrix* (1999) or the creation of entirely digital cast members in *Star Wars: Episode I – The Phantom Menace* (1999).

Digital technology had reached a maturity in power and performance. More importantly, the tools were in the hands of film-makers, animators and affiliated artists who brought the skills and understanding to harness that power. They were able to deliver photorealistic animation and special effects depicted environment, action and characters that were seamlessly integrated with the **live action**.

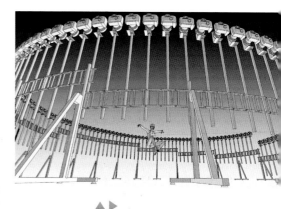

title
The Matrix

directors
The Wachowski Brothers

Bullet time was one of the many sequences that helped *The Matrix* win several awards for visual effects in 1999, including an Oscar and a BAFTA. It should also be recognised that in spite of the technology used, many established codes are present in the film. For instance, the technique of slowing down action to elevate critical elements can be traced as far back as the expressionist cinema of the 1920s.

Live action action in films involving filming real people or animals, as contrasted with animation or computer-generated effects.

Bullet-time sequence the illusion of extremely slow or frozen motion, achieved through computer-assisted blending of multiple still frames shot from an array of cameras.

Maturity

Bullet-time sequence

John Maeda's **bullet-time sequence** in *The Matrix* was a technique that created the illusion of time freezing while the camera tracked freely through the static world. While the technique had been used to varying degrees of success in television commercials, this was its first appearance in a cinematic feature.

In a reversal of the principles that Muybridge used to analyse movement, bullet time relies on arrays of still cameras, which are deployed along a line of action representing a movie camera path through a set. When the still cameras are triggered simultaneously the effect is to isolate perspective as an entity, so the only difference between each image is the view from each camera.

With images recorded, each frame was processed digitally for colour consistency and to correct problems of registration and distortion. The ideal frequency for still cameras could not be achieved because the physical size of the camera bodies dictated the distance between frames. In order to fill the gaps between each frame interpolation, software was used to generate the 'missing' frames in the same way a drawn animator would draw cels between key frames.

Only the actors were recorded with the still cameras. Since the sequence was duplicated digitally, the movement of the background could be animated to match on a separate plate or layer, and then composited to produce the final image.

Virtual actors

Star Wars: Episode I – The Phantom Menace saw George Lucas's return to the director's chair with an intent to unleash the full might of ILM to realise the epic vision of *Star Wars*. The arrival of digital technology allowed the scope to create Lucas's vision on a grand scale.

With an echo from the previous decade when ILM had married live action with drawn animation in *Who Framed Roger Rabbit* (1988), ILM embarked on creating the first fully digital lead character in a feature film without an exact plan of how to achieve it. The work done on *Jurassic Park* had substantially increased the level of realism of digital characters, but the decision to create a lead character that would interact and perform alongside live actors had never been attempted.

Of the several digitally animated characters seen in the film, Jar Jar Binks played the most prominent role, delivering a performance on a par with the human cast. The creation of the Binks model followed a path now established in digital character animation. Building the character model directly on screen with reference visualisations gives the geometry better accuracy than laser-scanning a maquette. The model's rig was designed around the performance requirements of the character, with emphasis on the facial controls needed for lip-synchronisation. A library of key expressions was also recorded before the package was delivered to digital animators.

title
**Star Wars: Episode I –
The Phantom Menace**

director
George Lucas

From the many innovations and advances in *The Phantom Menace* the realisation of a virtual actor is the most significant from a digital animation perspective. As well as demonstrating to the industry what could be achieved, the audience expectation of all future effects would be measured against this film.

Animation is not
the art of drawings
that move but the
art of movements
that are drawn.

Norman McLaren

The impact of digital technology at the beginning of the twenty-first century has made the production and delivery of animation easier than ever before. A general adherence to Moore's Law means the tools available to animators are increasingly sophisticated and powerful, producing spectacular and extraordinary imagery. Concurrently, embedded technology and standardisation allow novice animators a simple path into the field. Digitisation has democratised the making of media; digital cameras, digital music and the Internet mean the tools of production are now available at a domestic level.

With the complexity of computer systems discreetly embedded behind simple graphic user interfaces and friendly control panels, digital animation can be an intuitive process that is accessible to the non-technical and even the non-animator. Digitisation in diverse fields also means diversification for animation – from flashing LEDs on a microwave oven to a surgical training simulator. Digital animation is not only reaching new peaks of achievement, but broadening in its application.

title
MirrorMask

director
Dave McKean

Maturity > **Integration** > Predictions

At the start of the 21st century, the personal computer had become a fact of everyday life. In creative fields it had become ubiquitous. Graphic design, music and animation were made with, or adjusted by, digital tools. Computers were now able to rival broadcast standard video equipment. The increased efficiency of video compression tools and the gradual convergence of PC standards meant it was possible to custom build PCs with enough power to handle video editing, compositing and streaming duties. Studio equipment would be recognisable to the average domestic PC user.

As a result, the look of animation had changed accordingly. Not only did the use of digital tools result in a more stable, consistent and variable image – the movement of cameras and objects on screen could also be controlled by computer. With footage and still imagery in the same digital palette, the complexity and depth of combined media was only restricted by imagination, and video aesthetic had to evolve. Audiences were now used to complex computer games, live and animated television graphics, graphical screens for domestic appliances and mobile phones.

Historically, the production of animation has been conducted by patient people. The requirement for specialist equipment and media, the delay between shooting frames and processing film, even the laborious pre-roll, post-roll and cueing of analogue video tape recording, meant patience was always an important quality for animators. Digitisation has removed many time-consuming hurdles and hardware obstacles.

Social networking platforms

Pushed by the demand for accessibility, PC operating systems have become less technical and more stable allowing integration with the growing number of digital consumer electronic devices. The personal computer has left the office and laboratory, and become a central piece of domestic equipment, communication and entertainment.

The advent of popular networking for social and casual interaction through services like **MSN** and **MySpace** has also empowered individuals with access to a broadcast medium. **YouTube** has provided the missing component for many amateur and semi-professional film-makers and animators. Sites like these can be accessed for little or no financial outlay, and without the need to learn coding languages or design skills.

iStopMotion represents a dream come true for many a jaded animator and is a gift for anyone embarking on their first steps into animation. By linking a digital camera to a Mac, iStopMotion allows the capture of single frames of video with a simple key press. Changes between subsequent frames are immediately apparent, thanks to the 'onionskin' feature. A recorded series of images can be played back directly from the timeline to assess the animation as it is being recorded.

Integration

▲

title
iStopMotion

creator
Boinx Software

Tools like iStopMotion represent the democratisation of computer technology and the benefits of digitisation for amateur and professional animators. The simplicity of the interface allows the user to ignore the technology and concentrate on the animation.

Microsoft Network (MSN) the digital communication network offered by Microsoft providing its users with e-mail, messaging and news amongst other electronic media services.

MySpace website owned by News Corporation with the majority of its pages created by a network of individual contributors; a free stage for social networking and personal expression.

YouTube Google-owned website offering users an Internet facility for uploading and video-sharing. YouTube uses Flash technology to display the material from a searchable database to all Web users.

iStopMotion a digital animation tool offering animators a computer-based method of creating animation using traditional methodologies.

Digital tools for all > Digital feature films

Fan films

Fan films are those made by enthusiasts in tribute to, or as a parody of, existing commercial releases that have been made since the availability of domestic film-making equipment. The concurrence of digitisation, affordable equipment and a distribution medium – the World Wide Web – resulted in the fan film migrating from conventions and festivals into the public domain.

Armed with Mini DV cameras, Apple Macs and a suite of imaging software, Dave Macomber and Mark Thomas – The Crew of Two – were able to produce a six-minute short film that contained imagery and effects, which would only have been available to professional studios a decade previously.

Combining skills in design, martial arts and landscape painting, a pair of novice film-makers were able to create a convincing homage to the *Star Wars* saga. *Duality* emphatically demonstrates the dissemination of digital imaging technology and techniques into the wider public realm.

Highly intuitive tools such as Electric Image, **Adobe After Effects** and **Final Cut Pro** have allowed film-makers and animators to accomplish increasingly ambitious results through simplifying the technical process, and shortening the distance between the concept and outcome.

Integration

Adobe After Effects a software package from Adobe, which provides visual effects and motion graphics.

Final Cut Pro a digital non-linear editing software developed by Apple Inc.

▲ ◀

title
Duality

director
**Dave Macomber,
Mark Thomas
(The Crew of Two)**

The Crew of Two were able to
employ the same chroma-key
compositing and digital
animation techniques used in
mainstream cinema and
television production, with only a
basic knowledge of special
effects. The result, *Duality*, is
testament to the empowering
force of digitisation and its ability
to allow artists a route to realise
their visions without the inhibition
of restrictive technologies.

Digital tools for all > Digital feature films

Already proven by the accomplishments of various special effects sequences in mainstream feature films, digital technology had matured enough to be considered a medium for full-content production. Capitalising on the breakthroughs in CGI tools and the successful creation and reception of the first digitally animated feature, studios and production companies began to recognise the potential of computer animation as a viable form.

Imaging and animation computers were no longer just equipment added to the extended range of cinema technology because they were now directly in the hands of industry practitioners. In the case of animation, they became self-contained production facilities with the ability to accommodate the planning, execution and delivery of an animated film, all within the digital realm.

The arrival of the digitally animated feature film offered audiences an alternative to the established form represented by Disney and renewed interest in animation as a whole, both for audiences and as a possible medium for new animators and film-makers.

▲

title
Shrek

directors
Andrew Adamson and
Vicky Jenson

In occupying the ground traditionally held by and universally associated with Disney in terms of both animated features and fairytale subject matter, DreamWorks delivered a bold statement of intent.

▶

title
**Final Fantasy:
The Spirits Within**

director
Hironobu Sakaguchi

Final Fantasy remains a *tour de force* in terms of technical achievement and it rightfully occupies an important position in the history of animation.

Major studios and digital animation

The first computer-generated feature from DreamWorks, *Shrek* (2001), changed the way the film industry thought about computer animation. It took the scriptwriting potency of the television series, *The Simpsons*, and combined it with an irreverent humour reminiscent of classic Chuck Jones animation. Attracting adults and children in equal measure, the film's box office success seemed to be the signal for all major studios to consider their involvement in digital animation.

Taking a cue from the film's source – a children's picture book – the film's style followed a painterly approach with the colour palette and lighting designed to produce an impressionistic feel. Rendering techniques were developed to generate the flames and smoke, which were critical for the dragon character in the film. Custom CGI shaders coded for the donkey's fur, which were later adapted to create some of the grass and foliage in the film's rich environment.

Final Fantasy: The Spirits Within (2001) is another computer-generated feature, which was directed by Hironobu Sakaguchi. The film features a cast of talented voice artists, including Hollywood stars, and the backing of a major studio. Sony provided a purpose-built facility for the production of an incredibly advanced digital animation feature, which aimed to create the first photorealistic digital feature film.

In spite of all this, the film failed to sustain an audience. The technical execution of the animation brought the characters so close to being fully human that there is a legitimate question of why the film was not instead made with a real cast using digital environment and locations – the technology was certainly there to achieve such an undertaking. Audiences have also reported that there is a discomforting and unnatural feeling accompanying the virtual humans.

Digital auteurism

A significant outcome of the democratisation offered by the digitisation of media is the utilisation of digital animation to gather and repurpose disparate media to present new forms.

The common language offered by digitisation allows for an opportunity to juxtapose any sound, moving image or otherwise. As well, these tools are available in user-friendly forms, which enable artisans with little or no technological training to use them successfully.

Accessibility and media compatibility have provided artists with an unlimited palette and the chance to experiment with the languages and conventions accompanying a diverse array of media and disciplines.

The aesthetics of early computer-generated imagery dominated how people thought of digital images for many years. Wireframes, mechanical movement and the shiny plastic look of early computer graphics became the nemeses for CGI practitioners and developers, with a crusade for photorealism dominating mainstream work in special effects and animated features. It can be said that the race for photorealism has been won, as special effects teams can now measure the success of their work in terms of how invisible it is when used discreetly in a live-action feature.

Conversely the graphic qualities afforded by computer-generated or computer-manipulated images have also been embraced and enhanced by animators and studios to produce hybrid films and animation, which include not just moving picture convention, but aesthetic codes and generic conventions from other visual forms.

Accessible tools and software

Johnny Hardstaff's film, *Future of Gaming* (2001), represents many aspects of digital animation. Creating the piece without the use of digital tools would have required the use of a rostrum camera, compositor, sound engineering, photographers and film editors working in crews on a prohibitive time scale. In reality, the bulk of the artwork was prepared using tools available to the average PC user. In spite of the migration to a professional basis in the latter stages of the production, the film is representative of what can be achieved with affordable equipment and software.

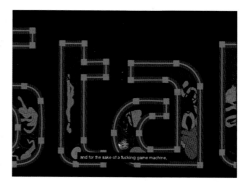

and for the sake of a fucking game machine.

The following is Johnny Hardstaff's account of the making of *Future of Gaming*:

'Working almost exclusively in Photoshop and Illustrator I generated all of the multi-layered composite artwork, creating multiple frames much as one might work in cell animation, saving each one, and then "glueing" them together in Autodesk Flame Software.

'I opted to use more domestic software for design. The material and my alleged skill in this field had ironically attracted the big production companies, and with them came the high-end and previously inaccessible kit.

'I had one assistant for some of the production period to help me generate artwork for the film, but otherwise I crafted almost every element. Hence, the three-to-four-month production period. For the first time, I also had access to an experienced and engaging editor (JD Smyth) who brought a strong dynamic to the film and improved it dramatically.'

The digital animator, working with significantly fewer tools than big studios and institutions, now has access to and control over the same imagery and aesthetic, thanks to the digitisation of media and the democratisation of the technology.

▼

title
Future of Gaming

director
Johnny Hardstaff

The diverse range of media now available and the ease with which they can be utilised evolves the language of film and video by juxtaposing diverse syntaxes and conventions, resulting in projects such as the *Future of Gaming*.

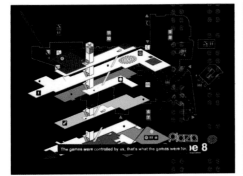

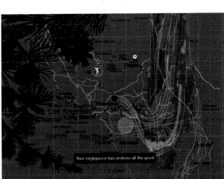

◀ ▲ ▶

title
**Constructed Passage –
Being Elsewhere**

animator
Christin Bolewski

*Constructed Passage - Being
Elsewhere* is a 52-minute
experimental video artwork
based on documentary footage.
It was assembled and
manipulated in a genre mix of
narrative and documentary film,
music clip and digital animation
using the 'cut and paste'
function of the computer to
create image and sound
sampling. The result is
a fragmented, rhythmic,
audiovisual pattern, which
dominates the structure of
the video.

Manipulating reality

Christin Bolewski is an artist whose work illustrates digital technology's capacity to integrate analogue material, including archive film, sound recordings and still photography, while still being self-exploratory in presenting the differences in old and new media technology.

The use of digital animation to assemble archive material not only presents the content in a new way, but exposes the nature of moving image technology and its effect on how images are received. Bolewski talks about her work, which involves reworking cinematic language and manipulating reality, as is evident in her film *Constructed Passage – Being Elsewhere* (2001):

'As a new media artist I am exploring digital animation and manipulation techniques to recreate cinematic language, and to develop innovative principles of montage and collage in time-based narration. I change and make abstract the content, tonality, expressivity of images and sounds through the process of digital collage, filtering and processing. I aim to reduce and reinterpret the information of the original footage to create distinctive artwork, which articulates my individual viewpoint.

'Having a strong affinity to documentary film practice, but knowing that each cut in film montage is already a lie, I use digital collage to emphasise my artistic intervention and to make the process of manipulation transparent for the viewer. I do not only assemble images in a linear fashion, I often use the concept of spatial montage to add a second layer of montage in a multi-layered stream of different media sources combining moving and still image, sound and animated text.

'Inspired by the conceptual idea of the audiovisual "counterpoint" of Sergei Eisenstein that montage should create new juxtapositions and collisions to unfold a complex narrative, I create a clash of disparate materials and viewpoints to articulate a postmodern position, where my voice as an artist is constructed through an impact of multiple sources of our information society.

'I do all digital image, sound processing and montage by myself to create an individual artistic expression. My practice mirrors the development of a lot of different production tools, and today I use mostly domestic software to generate multi-layered composite artwork. These tools are available for every artist, which makes us independent from big production budgets. In fact, the use of digital animation has increased enormously over the last few years in fine art practice and can be seen in a lot of independent art productions.'

▶

title
Constructed Passage – Being Elsewhere

animator
Christin Bolewski

The power and availability of digital tools have made it possible for artists to combine moving images with traditional media, creating new forms and combinations.

Integration

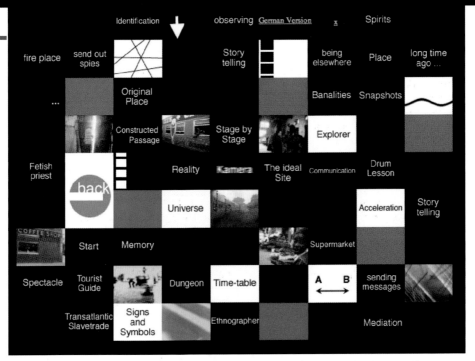

		Identification		observing	German Version	x	Spirits	
fire place	send out spies			Story telling		being elsewhere	Place	long time ago ...
	...	Original Place				Banalities	Snapshots	
		Constructed Passage		Stage by Stage			Explorer	
Fetish priest		back		Reality	Kamera	The ideal Site	Communication	Drum Lesson
			Universe				Acceleration	Story telling
	Start	Memory				Supermarket		
Spectacle	Tourist Guide		Dungeon	Time-table		A ←→ B	sending messages	
	Transatlantic Slavetrade	Signs and Symbols		Ethnographer			Mediation	

Reworking cinematic language and manipulating reality

Based on Christin Bolewski's works and advice, think of ways in which to develop digital collages to emphasise artistic intervention and to make the process of manipulation transparent for the audience. Experiment by using various types of film, narrative constructions, music clips and 2D or 3D animation to create a unique and artistic statement. Bolewski advises generating a multi-layered composite artwork. Use the concept of spatial montage to add another layer in a multi-layered stream of different media sources; combine moving and still images, sound and animated text. Try to create a work from disparate materials in order to come up with a unique voice and message.

Media digitisation has simplified the transfer of content in all forms between disciplines. The standardisation of formats at consumer and professional levels has transformed the mixing of media types into a simple exercise. Because digitisation is also occurring outside of media industries, links between previously separate industries are now appearing.

The growth of the computer games industry and the complexity and scale of individual games have resulted in a production process mirroring many of the practices of the film industry. Apart from the direct transfer of data between the forms, games share several philosophical and practical disciplines with film-making.

Games developers are adopting many cinematic techniques both on a practical and philosophical level. It is therefore not surprising that some games are based on films and vice versa. In the same way as a classically made animation project or live-action film would include pre-production stages of research, narrative planning, character development and production design, the industrial scale of many games projects now requires the same level of attention.

For example, in *Lara Croft: Tomb Raider* (2001), the back story and character development for the game series have produced an iconic figure, one who is strong enough for the development of a film franchise and several other media. The following are other examples where various media and platforms merge and cross over.

Games as educational tools

America's Army has a resonance with the adaptation of the *Battlezone* game in the early 1980s. It was originally developed on the game engines of *Doom* and *Rainbow Six*. The Internet-based multi-player game is comparable to many commercial software titles in terms of size and sophistication.

As technological advances are made in actual weapons systems, the use of games software to educate and inform a target audience has become an appropriate method for information dissemination and education. *America's Army* is not primarily a **simulator**; the game has grown from its roots as a training tool into an effective method of propaganda and advertisement. *America's Army* presents aspects of modern army activities and the codes by which the practice of warfare is conducted. It is an engaging game that combines realistic environmental graphics and accurate simulation, and has become a successful public relations and industrial recruitment tool.

▶

title
America's Army

project originator/director
Colonel Casey Wardynski

Rather than adopting the open chaos of many shooter games, *America's Army* requires the player to earn the right to engage in battle environments by completing basic training.

Digital auteurism > Media crossover > Aesthetic confidence

Simulator a virtual environment or mechanism that mimics actuality. Simulators were originally designed for training purposes, but have provided the basis for computer games.

Games based on films

The use of a **production bible** is important to maintain consistency in animated projects. This includes style guides and references that define the look of environments or objects; the motivation of characters is also used to maintain consistency and continuity. As games technology improves, the skills of animators must expand accordingly to include the more defined levels of characterisation. The convoluted route of a game based on a toy, based on a film series could end up bearing little resemblance to the original source material.

For example, the use of models created for animation purposes in *Star Wars* can be used directly for the creation of games titles based on the series. These can also be translated to create dies for manufacturing toys and miniatures.

Careful design and skillful animation using existing digital tools reproduce the look and feel of the *Star Wars* universe, and manage to imbue the game sprites with individual traits and mannerisms identifiable with the original characters in the films.

You can say a lot with pictures.
It's a visual medium – and especially with animation, you can do a lot that you can't do in live action.

Craig McCracken

◄▲

title
Clone Wars

director
Genndy Tartakovsky

The degree of control and detail in games has progressed to the point where the animation of games characters require a performance equivalent to film or theatrical acting. This is natural territory for animators working with techniques developed in stop-frame, drawn and digital character animation.

Production bible an archive of information containing the conventions of a film or series. Crew may refer to the production bible for information, such as character design, colour palette or scales of environments and props.

Digital auteurism > **Media crossover** > Aesthetic confidence

Aesthetic confidence

A dominant driving force in the development of digital animation and computer imaging has been a quest for photorealism to match the established forms of traditional animation. At the turn of the millennium, digital tools became sufficiently powerful and accessible, and audiences accepted that digital animators had latitude and confidence to explore a wider palette.

Rather than reproducing and mimicking drawn or stop-frame styles, digital animators could experiment with the capabilities of computer imagery and animation, creating movement and forms either impossible or impractical in other media.

The freedom offered by digital production includes flexibility over design, which can allow direct influence from, and easier integration with, other media especially since so many diverse media are also produced or assembled using digital tools.

The end result is a diverse range of animation, which has a uniquely digital aesthetic or strong influence from other fields such as graphic design, music, sculpture, manga, etc.

▼ ▲ ▶

title
Pocoyo

animator
Zinkia Entertainment

The innovative style of *Pocoyo* comes from developing traditional elements from traditional forms of animation using digital tools to incorporate codes and values from other visual media. The result is a form that continues the evolution of animation.

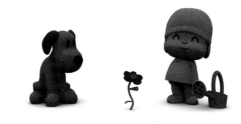

Integration

Digital animation in a pre-school television series

Zinkia's pre-school television series exploits the power of digital animation to produce a unique look and feel. The simplistic aesthetic belies the attention to detail and control of all aspects of the animation. Borrowing from several traditional sources, including live-action film, stop-frame, anime and storybook illustration, *Pocoyo* evokes instant familiarity, but has an entirely new feel to its aesthetic.

Pocoyo was designed specifically not to look like conventional 3D animation. The use of global illumination and matte textures is reminiscent of clay rather than CGI, delivering a tactile look to the production. The character design is deliberately targeted at a pre-school audience yet the minimal detail and simple design disguises a complex model and rig capable of portraying a huge range of expressions and actions.

Alberto Gontán, a member of the Press and Communications department for Zinkia, says that fundamentally, *Pocoyo* is a conceptually different production with a high educational content and 3D animation based on acting and exhaustive attention to detail. Detail is key to supplying each character with its own personality. Individual characters are carefully crafted to allow an immediate emotional and visual identification on the part of the viewer.

Directing animators

The direction of actors is very similar to the direction of animators. As can be seen in the case of *Pocoyo*, the director must have a global knowledge of the series and also an individual style and personality to give the programme its distinction. It helps greatly if directors are also excellent actors with a clinical eye. They must possess the subtlety and capacity for management and communication in order to transmit the necessary details to the animators, as well as keep the production in check.

Media crossover > Aesthetic confidence > Beyond cinema and television

Classic cinema with digital animation

With an agenda to create a true **hybrid** feature film with the production values of classic cinema, the creative team for *Renaissance* (2006) capitalised on the opportunities presented by digital technology to create science fiction drama with ambitious goals. The result is a visually unique animation, which incorporates futurist and expressionist aesthetics while maintaining the subtlety and detail to allow sympathetic performances from its cast.

The director, Matthieu Delaporte, talks in detail about the making of *Renaissance*:

'Paris is effectively a character in its own right in the film. On the one hand, we attributed it with almost human characteristics. The city is dark, twofold, changing… it is omnipresent in the film and in history. It is the perfect reflection of the evolution of the principal character, Karas, and the evolution of the universe. Paris is not a **futuristic** city. What interested us therefore was to reinvent modernity into an old city and represent visually the sociological and cultural changes to come.

'With regards to the role of animation in the writing, the fact that the film was in animation enabled us to give free course to our imagination. Everything was possible architecturally. The absence of problems with casting actors liberated us, and Karas could be conceived with complete freedom.

Hybrid something made by combining two different elements.

Futuristic a work of art set in the future, typically in a world of advanced or menacing technology.

'With the development of digital technology in live action film, I believe that one moves more and more towards a hybrid cinema – cine-animation – a cinema where the boundaries will become increasingly fuzzy.'

When a future vision of Los Angeles was required for *Blade Runner*, Douglas Trumble relied on physical miniatures and optical techniques supported by digital technology to render a convincing cityscape. In creating *Renaissance*, the digital tools allowed a wider palette with the physical elements used at the core of production during the **motion-capture** process.

▼

title
Renaissance

director
Christian Volckman

Set in the year 2054, *Renaissance* delivers a vision of the near future that is anchored in the recognisable features of present-day Paris.

Motion-capture the recording of movement using a computer. Usually achieved by tracking points on a moving body, motion capture (mocap) records movement in terms of vectors and time, allowing the motion to be displayed as wireframe or applied to third-party geometry.

Radio plays digitally realised

A quarter of a century after the original radio play and two decades from the television series, digital animation technology and techniques developed to a point where Douglas Adams's imagined universe could be realised in the feature-film production of *The Hitchhiker's Guide to the Galaxy* (2005). Of several scenes realised by Cinesite, the Planet Factory demonstrates the ability of computer-derived imagery to portray the impossible.

With so many areas of animation and film production requiring digital processing, it may appear on the surface that digital techniques and technology are dominant. In reality, the balance of expertise and specialist disciplines are still present, but new tools have been acquired.

With feature-film production now including specialist departments, the field of visual effects has broadened to the point where separate expertise may be sourced from separate studios on the same production or even the same shot. Directors must have a firm grasp of digital techniques or rely on a visual effects supervisor in order to translate and realise their vision.

Thrain Shadbolt, the 3D Sequence Supervisor at Cinesite, talks about the production process involved in the making of *The Hitchhiker's Guide to the Galaxy* and the crucial relationship between directors and visual effects supervisors:

'At Cinesite we have a pretty good mix of generalists and specialists, who provide a high degree of flexibility. We tend to work with people's specific talents and usually they tend to be best in one area. Very few people are really good at everything.

'We work with directors with a varying range of knowledge of visual effects. It is usually the visual effects supervisor on a production who is our key contact and "client". It is their job to understand the technical stuff, and to interpret it and deal with it on behalf of the director. Visual effects supervisors are the key liaison between the visual effects staff on the shop floor and the director. It is certainly not unusual for visual effects artists never to meet the director.

'*Hitchhiker's Guide* was certainly an exception. The director and producer were based so locally and had quite a high level of involvement. Technical knowledge isn't really necessary in a director, but dealing with directors who are enthusiastic and engaged by what we do is certainly the best scenario.'

Integration

◀

title
The Hitchhiker's Guide to the Galaxy – *movie*

director
Garth Jennings

The matte painting projection covers the entire panoramic camera move throughout the shot. Die-hard *Hitchhiker*'s fans might appreciate the subtle tribute in the background element. The 'head planet' is actually Douglas Adams, a likeness created from a 3D scan made before he died.

Media crossover > **Aesthetic confidence** > Beyond cinema and television

Matching techniques

With the television series *Firefly* (2002), Joss Whedon created a hybrid vision of the future that is concurrently exotic and familiar – a duality that runs through the entire production. Combining generic-form westerns and science fiction drama, Whedon's verse is both fantastic and conventional.

To remain sympathetic to the rhythm and atmosphere of the live action, Zoic Studios produced special effects sequences that matched the frenetic and irregular camera movements. These 'matching' techniques began in the 1990s to break with the 'locked off' camera feel from the days of physical matte paintings and optical compositing.

By 2002, digital animation facilitated matching the movement of live-action cameras. However, the visual effects in *Firefly* went beyond this matching technique by recreating the visual feel of hand-held cameras, not just in terms of stability, but by mimicking the aesthetic qualities of newsreel or war reportage.

Shots were composed in a vérité style despite being entirely produced as computer-generated sequences. Partial framing, 'manual' zooms and lagging focus pulls gave the look and feel of a shoulder-mounted camera shooting live action.

▶

title
Firefly

creator
Joss Whedon

The level of innovation in *Firefly* had previously only been attempted in feature-film production with feature-film budgets. The fact that such sophistication and high production values were attempted in a television series is indicative of the expansion and proliferation of digital imaging tools.

◀

title
Serenity

creator
Joss Whedon

Fundamentally, the digital animation for an episode of *Firefly* and sequences in *Serenity* are comparable and similar. The modelling, rendering and compositing went through similar stages and the final results are convincing in their juxtaposition with live-action footage.

Media crossover > Aesthetic confidence > Beyond cinema and television

Realistic aerial warfare

Double Negative is a London-based visual effects company working at the highest level of mainstream cinema production. With commissions for projects as varied as the film adaptation of *Doom* (2005) to the realistic *Billy Elliot* (2000), the range of services that were once the preserve of companies such as Industrial Light and Magic or Pacific Data Images are being delivered at the highest specification by a broad community of professional facilities.

For the period war film *Flyboys* (2006), Double Negative was tasked with a roster of visual effects to convey realistic aerial warfare during The First World War. With requirements that included digital treatment of live action to entirely CGI full simulations, Double Negative employed tools and techniques covering the spectrum of digital technology.

Innovative digital cameras designed by Panavision to match the look, feel and performance of film cameras were used to record live action, including green-screen studio work. To create accurate flight simulations, accelerometer-based motion capture was used to record actual flight manoeuvres – data that was mapped on to digital replicas of period planes.

A combination of techniques was used, including custom-built software, to simulate various environments and effects, such as clouds. The digital props were deployed to enhance the portrayal of speed and location, using visual markers in relation to the fighter planes.

◀ ▲

title
Flyboys

director
Tony Bill

With an array of established techniques and the ability to perform research and development on individual projects, companies such as Double Negative represent the next generation of digital effects professionals. Working with the same mandates as the original pioneers, they are adding to the palette and toolkit of digital animation and effects.

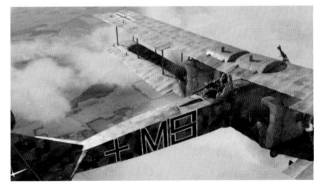

Digital compositing

More and more artists and animators work with a variety of media to produce distinctive and compelling imagery. Dave McKean is such an artist and composes artwork from a variety of sources: drawings, paintings, photography and calligraphy are assembled digitally to create atmospheric and emotive artwork. Digitisation has enabled the transition of his work and vision from the page into animation and interactive forms.

It is with the benefit of an eclectic palette and broad view of media technology that McKean was able to realise *MirrorMask* (2005) as a feature film. The fantasy tale is co-written with long-term collaborator, Neil Gaiman. It is heavily reliant on digital compositing and animation technologies to produce environments and characters, which display elements of sculpture, surrealist art, silhouette puppetry and early cinema.

Dave McKean lists the advantages of making films and his work method:

'Working in film, the biggest gains are sound and music – the subtleties of real actors and the power of motion and sound combined; it gives you a full sensory experience. I'm especially interested in telling stories that take place in an inner world of the mind – dreams and thoughts, the past and future, the real and the imagined versions of reality. I'm not bothered about genre, or whether the films are short, long, commercial or art. Just whether I'm involved in the characters' ideas, and whether these ideas can be expressed in exciting ways.'

I prefer that animation reach into places where live action doesn't go, and it seems like all of animation nowadays is trying to go where live action is.

Don Bluth

▲

title
MirrorMask

director
Dave McKean

MirrorMask possesses qualities apparent in Victorian peep shows, Svankmajerian animation and theatrical melodrama. The hallmarks of McKean's illustrative work have migrated seamlessly to feature-film form.

Descending costs of computer technology and miniaturisation have seen video and computer technology become embedded in devices other than television and cinema equipment. The adaptability of a VDU screen has replaced control panels in many instances, thanks to the introduction of smaller LED and LCD displays, and the integration of touch screens.

With increasing screen resolution and expanded functionality discreetly built into devices, the design of controls and interfaces has necessarily required further skills for the industrial designer, which includes animation. Following a similar pattern of development as the computer interface, complex (and often not-so-complex) technology that once would have required the study of an operation manual can now have instructions built into it. Instructions can be displayed using animated icons or even video on the same screen, which converts into a panel of buttons.

Digital technology has also migrated into large-format display systems. Matrices of lights are now replacing the neon advertisements in Times Square and Piccadilly, while banks of LEDs are programmed to display messages in sports stadia. Proliferation has allowed digital imagery and animation to become ubiquitous tools in fields ranging from architecture to science.

As Internet speeds increase and access to the Web grows, a new opportunity for exhibition has arrived for an audience who are also all potential makers and exhibitors of digital animation.

▲ ▶

title
Inanimate Alice

animator
Kate Pullinger, Babel, Ian Harper

Scrolling a screen of information is familiar to anyone who has used a modern computer or surfed Web pages. By adding a small bounce and deceleration to the end of a scrolled list, the iPhone user is given an extra visual reference signifying that the end of the list has been reached.

Portable electronic devices

Mobile phones, **personal digital assistants (PDA)** and even small pieces of equipment previously not associated with electronic technology now incorporate bespoke graphic user interfaces for general use. Where once an indicator light may have been sufficient warning that a battery is low on power, now an illuminated LCD will display the exact percentage of power left in a radio or drill.

When used correctly, animation can help with the reading of complex devices. The advent of **global positioning systems (GPS)** and navigation systems not only makes the viewing of a map simple and adaptable, allowing the amount of detail or information to be adjusted by the reader, but it also simulates the journey with a live perspective view of the road ahead. The information design of such a complex tool exploits the same techniques of in-betweening and movement used in animation for camera moves and timing action.

The use of animation techniques in the design of a telephone is not an immediate association for most people, including animators. However, as the range of functions available to the user increases, so the interface between the person and the device must develop. In the case of the **iPhone**, functionality is intuitive and natural, relying as it does on technology and familiar cues.

The motion graphics used in the touch-screen interface are not embellishments to promote the performance of the contained technology, but rather carefully choreographed cues that assist the user to navigate through the functions and virtual topology of the information. Small enhancements make it easier to understand what is happening in various operations.

Personal digital assistant (PDA) a hand-held electronic device for storage and collation of personal information.

Global positioning system (GPS) a digital navigational system based on triangulation with satellite signals.

iPhone Apple's combined mobile telephone, iPod and Internet device, which employs a screen-based user interface.

Aesthetic confidence > Beyond cinema and television

Chemical modelling

Computer-aided design (CAD) is well known for its application in pre-visualising expensive projects for architects and film-makers. In specialist areas of research, academia and industry are exploiting the increased performance of digital technology, which has allowed significant improvement in visualisation techniques. The simulation and visualisation of chemical structure has migrated from a physical modelling activity to a virtual technique. Dr Stephen Walker, a health and sport psychologist, comments on the advantages and significance of animation in computational modelling:

'Traditionally, physical 'ball-and-stick' models have been used to demonstrate the conformational properties of molecules. For small molecules, physical models offer a convenient way of visualising their overall shape and the connectivity between atoms. However, the availability of computer animation for molecular modelling holds a number of advantages over physical model kits.

'Computational modelling allows the tailoring of geometric properties, such as bond lengths and angles. Physical models can only ever give an idealised view of the molecule, in which these parameters are uniform. In reality, the nature of the atoms and their connectivity can lead to significant deviation from the idealised model.

'The combination of computer-generated models with algorithmic methods, such as energy minimisation, is at the forefront of many computational chemistry techniques, as well as in the analysis of experimental data and prediction of various physical properties. Such techniques allow the simulation of chemical reactions, predict the efficacy of drug molecules, and the determination and prediction of crystal structures.'

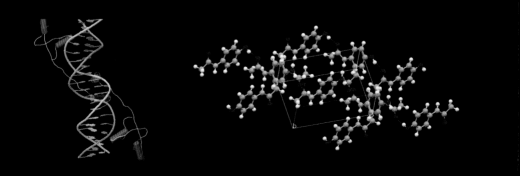

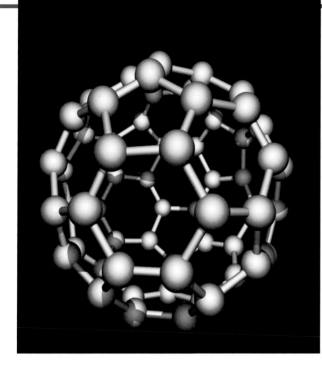

title
**JMol haemoglobin
visualisation, DNA molecule,
Fullerene molecule**

courtesy of
Dr Steven Walker

The building of 'ball-and-stick'
models become impractical as
larger, more complex structures,
such as biomolecules, are
considered. Computer models
(such as the ones illustrated) can
be constructed relatively quickly
to represent structures
containing thousands of atoms.
They can also be displayed with
various degrees of complexity.

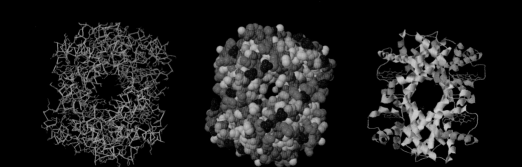

Concerts and music tours

The platform for innovative technology and the array of media found in a rock music show can often range from lighting effects to cinematic projection. The U2 Vertigo Tour (2005) included elements as disparate as drawn animation, CGI, live feeds from SMS messaging and kites! Providing much of the animation, graphic design and video content was Onedotzero Industries. At the centre of the operation was award-winning show designer Willie Williams, who gives an insight into the complexity and variety of tasks in realising such a colossal undertaking:

'The initial phase of the design process sees the first meeting of ideas between the designer and the client. Usually the process is reactive on the part of the client. The designer presents sketches – three or more quite different ideas, so the client has something to respond to. This dialogue between performer and designer will steer the evolution of the design; in the case of U2 they will remain closely involved at every stage of the journey.

'A rock show is unique in that it is the only kind of staged performance without a director. Performers have the final say, which in one sense makes them "the director". They are also funding the operation, which technically makes them the producer as well. Ironically, the performer is the only person unable to watch the show in context, so having confidence in the design team is paramount.

'Placing myself between the touring video and lighting directors, I controlled certain aspects of the selection and playback of video sequences, as well as parts of the lighting system. By collecting footage at each show, we were able to assemble some interesting short films of the performance.

'The video control system was built for the show involving a great deal of custom software and a visualiser, which allowed me to see what the show looked like from all angles. U2 will always need the freedom to wander from the "script", so many of the visual elements of the show can be pre-programmed, but the operation, cueing and timing always have to be manual. Besides, it's more fun to operate manually rather than just pushing the "go" button.'

Animation offers a medium of storytelling and visual entertainment, which can bring pleasure and information to people of all ages everywhere in the world.

Walt Disney

Integration

◀ ▲

title
U2 Vertigo Tour

designer
Willie Williams

The giant rear video screen of the Vertigo Tour's outdoor show housed an enormous lighting gallery containing twelve human 'follow spot' operators receiving verbal instructions from the lighting director.

Aesthetic confidence > Beyond cinema and television

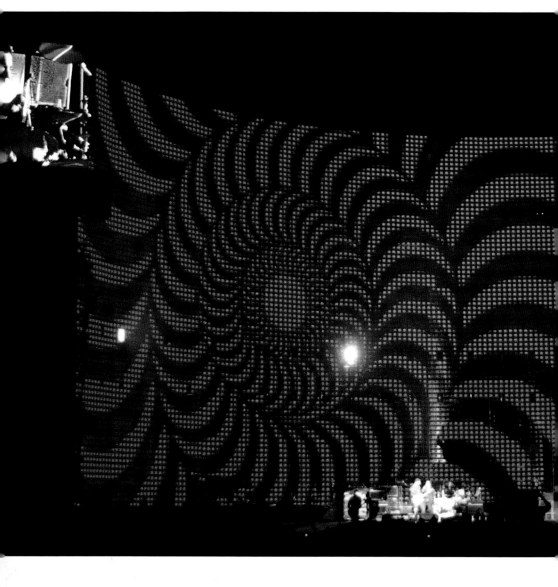

title
U2 Vertigo Tour

animator
Willie Williams

Digitisation of media production, from creation to delivery, has allowed such control and combination of sound and vision that live performance can rival the spectacle of post-produced film and video.

Show designers and production teams

According to Willie Williams, the show designer holds a somewhat nebulous position in concert production – partly because the designer often does not stay with the tour, but mostly because of the symbiotic relationship with the production team. In one sense, the designer represents the vision of the performer, and the production team exists solely to realise this vision. However, the designer is reliant on the production team to make things happen. In practical terms, the designer can achieve nothing without the continuous, dedicated assistance of the production manager and the entire touring crew. Mutual respect, combined with some sense of a common goal, is crucial to allow a tour to achieve its creative, logistical and financial goals.

Aesthetic confidence > Beyond cinema and television

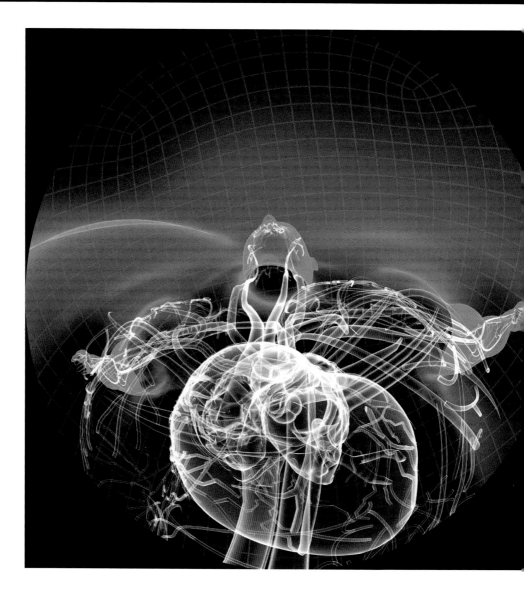

Planetaria

The flexibility of digital animation not only enhances, replaces and combines established media, but it has also evolved new forms that could not exist without CGI. Again, expensive development of specialist technology has been driven by industry and government. Flight simulators that date from the 1950s only attained a graphic display when computer technology had developed enough to allow rendering imagery in real time, and at a scale to fill a pilot's field of vision.

At the National Space Centre UK in Leicester, the creation of digital environments in its Space Dome employs the use of a variety of digital media, which create a new form of visual presentation.

◀

title
Microscopic simulation and human anatomical visualisation

courtesy of
National Space Centre UK

Illustrating the cutting edge of digital animation technology, the animated exploration of a human body includes the staple techniques of wireframe rendering and diagrammatic representation, but also has resonance with Da Vinci's study and depiction of human anatomy.

Max Crow of the National Space Centre lists the challenges of working with digital animation within a domed environment:

'There are disadvantages to the dome theatre format as you cannot use traditional techniques, such as cutting between action to create drama – the audience finds it too confusing. Instead, the scenes take a slower pace and can continue for several minutes before transitioning into the next. This makes the format ideally suited to science and space documentary, where the viewer can experience an unrestricted view whilst travelling over the surface of Mars, flying through a nebula or even swimming with dolphins, which television and IMAX cannot compete with.

'CG animation is the primary tool for dome production because as yet, conventional lenses and cameras cannot cope with the distortion; custom-rendering packages are used to convert scenes so that they can be projected on to the curved screen of a dome.

'Producing audio is another area of full-dome production in its infancy. Composers have to create sounds that complement the action in a way that goes beyond 5.1 stereo. The sound has to exist and move in three dimensions. This unique and exciting format brings a whole new way of experiencing audio and visual entertainment, and it will continue to grow as the animation tools get better and better.'

Aesthetic confidence > **Beyond cinema and television**

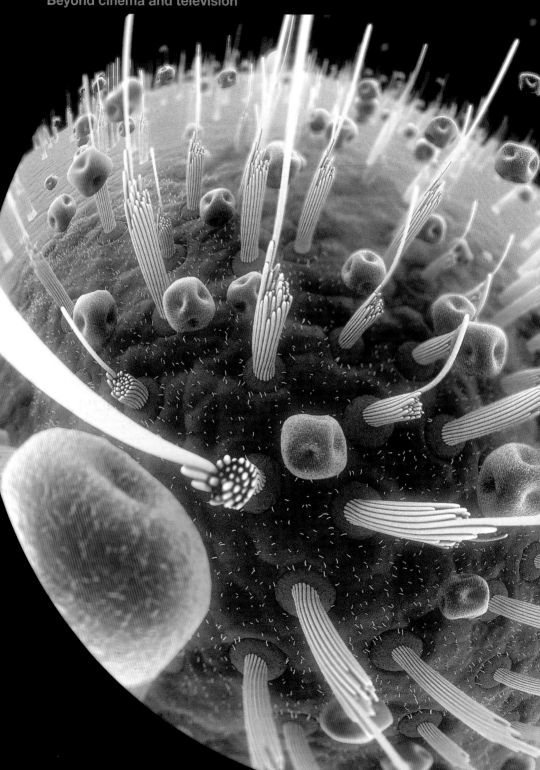

◀

title
Microscopic simulation and human anatomical visualisation

courtesy of
National Space Centre UK

The photorealistic quality of digital animation tools allows us to visualise images, which could not be achieved in any other way. The NSC Space Theatre exploits this power to take audiences into environments as extreme as outer space, or in this case to the microscopic confines of the human ear.

Audio for dome theatres

CG animation for dome theatres is a new discipline that bridges the gap between stage, television and IMAX. The images surround the audience with a 360-degree field of vision, giving them the choice of what to look at. In cinema and television, the images are projected on to a flat rectangle. In a dome theatre, the images are projected on to the side of a hemisphere – hence there is no frame or composition. Composers have to create sound that complements the action and exists in three dimensions.

Aesthetic confidence > Beyond cinema and television

caboose

As in the early days of cinema, the novelty of new technology and the spectacle of tricks and effects are not enough to sustain the medium. The familiarisation with computer technology and the gamut of digital animation and CGI mean that audiences demand more than effect and innovation. Animation must refocus on content and meaning, reviving the key values of film-making and the fundamentals of animation.

Digital tools have not only changed the way animation is made; they have also transformed attitudes towards animation. The impact of computer technology has forced the rapid evolution of animation in a multitude of ways.

At the leading edge of animation, in both industry and the arts, the increasing potency of computer technology means faster, more complex digital tools to create grander and more sophisticated animation. Concurrently, a broader group of professional and amateur animators have the benefits of simplified interfaces and more accessible technology.

The next generation of digital animation tools will inevitably be faster, easier to use and more potent. This will then re-establish the balance in animation practice between technical understanding and creative contribution, therefore increasing accessibility to a wider number of potential animators and giving greater reach to current practitioners.

title
Red vs Blue

creator
Rooster Teeth Productions

Integration > Predictions

Machinima

Machinima is a medium wherein both animation (CGI) and film-making techniques are used. It is representative of the potential for cross-media transfer due to proliferating digitisation. The ease with which video games allow the capture of 3D content in real time is one of the many advantages of machinima.

By exploiting the interactivity and sophistication of games consoles and software, machinima-makers are able to control characters, cameras, environments and props. The action is recorded as video source material, which can be edited into new narratives and scenarios.

After embracing the heritage from the game modding (game modification) and demoscene communities, 'machinimators' have been experimenting with the use of video games as creative tools since 1996. Machinima has moved from being an amateur yet effective technique to a medium used in online digital performances and VJing (video jockeying). The vocabulary and ambition of the form has grown to incorporate cinematic values and conventions resulting in narratives that transcend, and on many occasions subvert, the original material.

▲ ▶

title
Machinima Island

animators
Ricard Gras, Gareth Howell, Alex Lucas

Winner of the 2007 European Machinima Festival award for Best Technical Achievement, *Machinima Island* allowed artists with widely different backgrounds and skill sets to combine their talents and create a narrative film using the *Second Life* platform as a basis for production.

Machinima the practice of using games and other computer graphic media as the basis for creating new animation.

Role playing platforms

Machinima, in many ways, exemplifies the general state of digital animation. The available content is as wide as the imagination, but requires the animator to pay respect to the techniques beyond image-making: script, story, character and the established skills of film-making. In the case of machinima, however, the use of a commercial video game has specific cultural and artistic implications, which must be taken into account.

Second Life (an Internet-based virtual world) has foundations in games technology and an open, unscripted structure, offering a high degree of control to the machinima-maker. The **virtual world** allows participants to control almost every aspect of what appears on the screen, including the physical attributes of the characters, avatars to the objects, buildings and environments. *Second Life* can be used as a virtual theatre stage or film set, complete with actors and props.

Virtual world an environment that does not physically exist, but is made by computer software to appear similar to the real world.

New hybrid forms

Digital animation is usually rendered as individual frames before being assembled into a movie during film and television production. For complex imagery, there may be several renders for each frame resulting in individual components, which must be assembled or composited to form the finished image.

Since much of the technology powering games consoles is derived directly from personal computer technology, the benefits of increased performance and falling costs also drive the evolution of computer games hardware and software. Not only does the current generation closely resemble PCs in terms of operation and adaptability, but the level of video graphics and animation has edged closer to rendered animation and cinematic effects.

The *Red vs Blue* series is a true hybrid form that takes aspects of cinema, animation and puppetry to produce what is effectively a situation comedy. Fully acknowledging its roots, the series has acquired cult status with audiences from the gaming community, as well as animation, film and machinima followers. To disregard it because of its source material is to seriously miss the intent and sophistication of the production.

Far from being a departure from traditional forms, *Red vs Blue* is easily accessible to audiences as it respects conventions of film and television in terms of timing, cinematography and narrative structure. Its use of popular games gives the *Red vs Blue* episodes a peculiar set of connotations.

Studios have been trying to get rid of the actor for a long time and now they can do it. They got animation. No more actor, although for now they still have to borrow a voice or two. Anyway, I find it abhorrent.

James Coburn

▼ ▶

title
Red vs Blue

creator
Rooster Teeth Productions

Rooster Teeth Productions uses Halo by Microsoft Game Studios to create its *Red vs Blue* machinima series. Despite the limitations of resolution and characters with hidden faces, the story is driven by careful editing, strong voice artists and accomplished comedic writing.

Machinima > Return to core values

Return to core values

It has taken the maturity of digital animation technology, and an acceptance on the part of audiences, to allow a return to the fundamental concepts of animation. Spectacle and sensation alone do not sustain audience attention. The core concepts of narrative and character are essential and central to all film-making. They remain the basis for success whether working on commercial film, independent projects or experimental work.

While the pursuit of photorealism and seamless special effects have preoccupied many industrial practitioners, animators with traditional skills and motivations have recognised the potential of digital animation tools to create animation with even more timeless values embodying an individual voice or aesthetic.

The migration of digital animation tools from technologists to media professionals began the process of integrating established animation techniques. However, the proliferation and accessibility of computer imaging technology to individual animators has increased the diversity of digital animation aesthetics as experimenters and artists availed themselves of digital tools.

By respecting core values such as scriptwriting, timing, acting, design and characterisation, animators have demonstrated that the critical components of animation are the same as ever. With powerful imaging software requiring less technical training, digital animation has allowed the transfer of traditional skills from animators with roots in established areas of the medium, therefore confirming the place of digital animation in the extended family of the discipline.

Studio-based experimental animation

JoJo in the Stars (2003) is the work of Marc Craste, an animator responsible for some of the most stylistically refined and carefully observed animation made in any medium. The work was produced by Studio AKA, a studio with a growing reputation for experimental and innovative animation. *JoJo in the Stars* represents a departure from the established conventions of 3D computer graphics of authentic physics and photorealism. It received multiple awards, including the BAFTA for Best Animated Short in 2004.

JoJo in the Stars is successful partly because 3D CGI is secondary to the realisation of the work. Although many of the elements within the animation would have been difficult, if not impossible, to achieve in any other way, each component serves the design and delivery of the film-maker's vision without descending into spectacle. It achieved innovation and transcended its medium, not through exhaustive technical formalism, but through an appropriate use of available tools.

Character and set design were pared back to a minimum in the making of *JoJo in the Stars*, and only absolute story essentials were included. Elements such as staging, lighting and atmosphere all became as important as the animation in conveying the emotions and moods present in the film.

title
JoJo in the Stars

director
Marc Craste

Detail and technical hurdles were pared back in the making of *JoJo in the Stars*. However, the film does not suffer from this approach; instead, it allows for a focus on bringing the story to life.

Machinima > **Return to core values** > Digital auteurism revisited

Experimental animation – independent artists

Two Fellas (2005) by Dan Lane is another example that could be classified under the heading 'experimental animation'. Dan was one of the dozen UK-based animators involved in creating short films for SE3D – a project run by Watershed, Hewlett Packard and Alias. SE3D supplied animators with a full Maya licence and access to a high-end render farm in California, which had been employed by clients such as DreamWorks Animation.

Despite the technological prerequisites, Dan is a champion of the values and skills that animators from any era would recognise. Having studied, trained and worked in traditional drawn animation, Dan traversed several duties at Aardman Animations before joining their burgeoning digital department in 2000.

▼ ▶

title
Two Fellas

animator
Dan Lane

The backgrounds for *Two Fellas* were done in Mental Ray and the animation was all Maya-rendered. All the camera moves were done in post-production to save time, and the textures were developed in Photoshop.

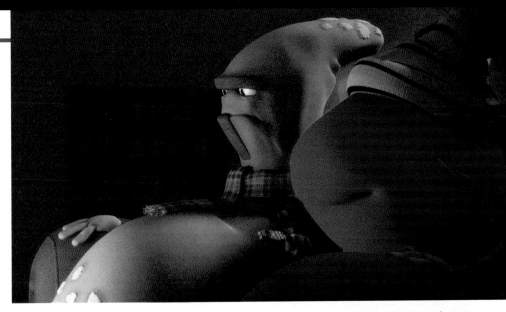

**Dan Lane's most important tools
for CG animation:**

A good traditional base
There is nothing like making horrendous mistakes on a
traditional piece that take hours, days or weeks to fix.
You learn to 'think first, animate second'. That should
apply to CG as well.

Good reference material
Keep all the things that have inspired you to animate,
including good animation handbooks such as those
from Disney, Richard William, Don Bluth and Preston
Blair. Films with good acting in them are also a useful
reference – for example, drama and comedy.

People with great ideas
There is little better than throwing ideas around with
friends, colleagues or peers. You can bounce ideas off
each other – it's the cheapest and quickest animation
there is. You can quickly spot what's not going to work.
If a set up really makes you laugh, it will probably make
others laugh too.

The common language offered by digitisation allows easy exchange and collaboration between disparate practitioners. Technically accommodating tools mean it is possible to manipulate sound and image with minimal instruction. However, this global accessibility has been misinterpreted with the term 'convergence'.

Experts and specialists are still present and necessary, and animators using digital tools are as diverse in motivation and technique as ever. Mastery of digital tools requires as much investment as any other discipline; acceptance of this fact by new media artists results in practices, which hybridise technique and language, resulting in innovative and challenging work.

In the same way that desktop publishing technology revolutionised an entire industry, the digitisation of film and video has changed animation production fundamentally. Similarly, the ease of access to animation technology also resonates with the associated pitfalls of technological accessibility.

Animation, like all film-making processes, is a balance of ideas and technique. When conceptual art-makers embrace the technological challenge of mastering digital tools the result is work expanding the scope of the medium, enhancing film and video language.

Animation is the most contemporary form of human expression, combining the elements of motion, storytelling, sound and space.

John Halas

Digital film-making

Fine art graduates of Central St Martins, Al and Al have adopted digital film-making as their medium, working collaboratively to assemble virtual characters and environments that are created and composited using television effects and graphics tools.

Using a **blue-screen** studio as a canvas to create films, their work is assembled using familiar terms, but in an unusual syntax. Aesthetics from broadcast television, games cut scenes and cinematic effects coexist with sculptural sensibilities, **surrealism** and **photomontage**, challenging the viewer not only to read the work, but also to question the media elements that have become so familiar. Al and Al provide an insight into their working method and their sources of inspiration:

◀

title
Interstellar Stella

animator
Al and Al

Al and Al's *Interstellar Stella* is a digital film created by using television effects and graphic tools.

'To date all our works have been conceived, performed, programmed, composited, edited, directed and produced by just the two of us in our own blue-screen studio. Although much of contemporary art is produced by technicians instructed by artists, we wanted to discover what the two of us could achieve together in a small, five-metre square studio space.

'When first using blue screen, we were very conscious of substituting real studio space for a blue-screen void, replacing the confines of the studio context for an infinity screen where we could build computer-generated contexts for the performances filmed later. We wanted the same freedom as a painter – to climb a mountain without going there, to jump off a building without a crash mat – this is how we got seduced into computer programming. Everything you see in our films has been made in our studio by us.

'The image we have made of *Stephenson's Rocket* landing on the Edge Hill moon makes reference to the world's first special effects film-maker, Georges Méliès, who in 1902 made the film, *Le Voyage dans la Lune*, which included a rocket ascending to the moon. The image represents for us the beginnings of technology's ultimate travel plans: leaving the planet.'

Blue screen a special-effects technique used in films in which scenes shot against a blue background are superimposed on other screens.

Surrealism a twentieth century avant-garde movement in art and literature, which sought to release the creative potential of the unconscious mind.

Photomontage a montage constructed from photographic images.

Return to core values > Digital auteurism revisited

Digital proliferation

The usability of professional level software has allowed its utilisation by once disparate practitioners. Michael Shaw represents a vanguard of artists who have discovered the potential of digital technology to expand the established boundaries of their traditional skills base. Michael believes that film and video have increasingly been championed as the zeitgeist of contemporary art, yet if one is not interested in figuration or literary narrative, then the media promise little.

He realised that animation could perhaps facilitate explorations of abstract kinetic forms. The latter was first intimated whilst exploiting CAD software to manufacture sculpture through rapid prototyping technologies. While in the learning stage, it soon became apparent to Michael that animation could not only be a powerful modelling tool, but also a dynamic means to create chameleonic sculptural form with the potential to continually metamorphose its geometry, material qualities, surface and colouration:

'The first frame of animation, as with drawing on to a blank page, is a kind of liberation because the sculptor can tentatively explore "what might be" without restriction. Furthermore, the potential for form generation in the digital realm seems amplified because axes of deformation can be subtly moved off-centre to destabilise the horizontal and vertical meridians and overall symmetry, whilst retaining the underlying unity of a form's gestalt. Similarly, the range of material qualities, surface finishes and colours appear almost endless too.

'Perhaps one of the most exciting aspects of digital animation is its capacity to tell a better lie! It has the ability to create the illusion of three-dimensional space on a flat plane. These are issues explored in all my films, but particularly in *There, But Not There*, which also references the act of drawing by effectively documenting its own creation. The continuous mapping of form through moving pencil lines is a surrogate drawing in space: a sculptural sketch of what might be "there, but not there".'

▶

title
Respiro I and Respiro II

animator
Michael Shaw

The ability of CAD software to sequentially save increments of activity and to infinitely duplicate, copy and paste are all particularly welcome technical additions to the lexicon of the traditional object-maker. These characteristics encourage playful and intuitive exploration.

Adobe Photoshop
A software application developed as a mass-market accessible tool for photographic enhancement and retouching.

Analogue
The use of variation in physical property to record or display information. For example, change in colour or tone creates a photographic image on film.

Animation
The discipline of representing movement, often broken into specialisms of mechanical effects and character animation.

Anime
Stylised Japanese animation influenced by manga; typically with science fiction fantasy and erotic themes.

Auteur
A film-maker who retains creative control over production, often creating an individual style in a work or series.

Blue screen
A special-effects technique used in films in which scenes shot against a blue background are superimposed on other screens.

Bullet time
The illusion of extremely slow or frozen motion, achieved through the computer-assisted blending of multiple still frames shot from an array of cameras.

Cels
Sheets of transparent celluloid traditionally used for drawn animation.

Chroma-key
The use of colour to mask or replace areas of video or film footage to add subsequent images during post-production.

Compositing
The addition or combination of several elements of imagery in the same sequence of film or video.

Computer-aided design (CAD)
The use of computer technology for the industrial production of artefacts at the design stage in order to aid visualisation and planning.

Computer-assisted animation
The use of digital technology to enhance or manipulate recorded material.

Computer-generated imagery (CGI)
Images that are originated within the digital environment.

Cut-scene
Sequences in computer games between sections of play where consequences of interactivity are portrayed or a narrative is developed.

Diegetic
Components of a film that exist in the narrative or created environment. For example, the sound of actors' voices are diegetic, but a narrator's voice-over is non-diegetic.

Digitisation
The conversion of information or media into binary form; a translation into 1s and 0s, thus recognisable to computers and digital technology.

Dope sheets
A chart used to disseminate information to the production crew by breaking the information down into columns of data. The centre of production for animation, it is the analogue ancestor of the timeline found in digital video applications.

Easing
An animator's technique to control motion; accelerating and decelerating the beginning and end of a movement.

Expressionism
A style in which the artist seeks to express the inner world of emotion rather than external reality.

First-person shooter (FPS)
A video game genre where the player interacts in a virtual environment with the point of view of the active character.

Flash
Software released by Adobe in the mid 1990s as a vector-based animation and interactive content package for the Internet.

Flying rig
A mechanical support for objects in stop-frame animation, usually puppets, where the action requires an unbalanced or airborne pose.

Hardware
The physical components of digital technology, from mechanical to electronic.

Hologram
A three-dimensional image formed by the interference of light beams from a laser or other coherent light source.

Industrial Light & Magic (ILM)
George Lucas's assembled team of talented crafts people originally founded in 1975 to help realise his vision for *Star Wars*.

Interactive
The ability for a system to be affected by user control. Computer game technology is an example of an interactive medium.

iStopmotion
A digital animation tool offering animators a computer-based method of creating animation using traditional methodologies.

Key frame
The point of significant change in an animated sequence.

Live action
Action in films involving filming real people or animals, as contrasted with animation or computer-generated effects.

Machinima
The practice of using games and other computer graphic media as the basis for creating new animation.

Manga
The generic Japanese term for printed comics. Manga is a major source of themes for anime.

Maquette
A sculptor's small preliminary model or sketch.

Marathon series
A benchmark for the FPS genre of games. It was a series that shared many aspects of film-making, with considerable attention to detail in the creation of environmental graphics, sound effects and character design. It had a strong narrative structure and a realistic feel.

Marsha effect
The corruption or deletion of data or imagery through the inappropriate imposition of protocols, usually precipitating syntax errors or system failure.

Matching techniques
Where digital animation mimics the movement of live action cameras.

Matte painting
An image used to depict, enhance or modify the environment of a film sequence. Original matte paintings were physical objects placed in front of cameras and filmed live to obscure and replace an element of the frame. Modern versions may be digitally created and added live or in post-production.

Modelling (computer)
The virtual construction of objects, environments and characters using digital tools.

Motion capture
The recording of movement using a computer. Usually achieved by tracking points on a moving body, motion capture (mocap) records movement in terms of vectors and time, allowing the motion to be displayed as wireframe or applied to third party geometry.

Motion control
The use of computer technology to control a crane, rig or other articulated camera mount to move a camera through a specified path with the ability to repeat the movement accurately and identically.

Multiplane rostrum
A camera invented by the Disney Studios. It is mounted above several layers of artwork, which can be manipulated independently to enhance the illusion of three-dimensional space.

Non-linear
A system that allows sequences of filmed footage to be arranged or rearranged in any order. Legacy analogue formats of video editing required the consecutive assembly of sequences.

Onionskin
The ability to see a number of frames of artwork in a sequence concurrently. Originally derived from backlighting drawn paper cels to see pencil lines, onion-skinning in digital animation allows the animator to display several stored frames on screen.

Optical printer
A mechanical tool for compositing pre-filmed elements on to a single film strip. The analogue device is a camera which re-shoots multiple films on to a combined 'master'.

Oscilloscope
An electronic testing device displaying visual interpretation of voltage or current using light trace to show lines and waveforms.

Photomontage
A montage constructed from photographic images.

Photorealism
The practice of creating artwork that is photographic in appearance. Photorealism is a dominant concern for simulation and invisible film effects where imagery is required to imitate real environments or match existing filmed material.

Pixilation
A form of stop-frame animation that uses people and actors as puppets or props.

Post-production
The part of film-making between the point at which footage has been recorded and the creation of the final edited version.

Praxinoscope

An early mechanical device that produced the illusion of movement in a similar way to the zoetrope. The praxinoscope allows the viewer to watch a series of images mounted on the inside of a spinning cylinder. The restricted view gives an illusion of continuos movement via a series of mirrors on the axle of the spinning cylinder.

Production bible

An archive of information containing the conventions of a film or series. Crew may refer to the production bible for information such as character design, colour palette or scales of environments and props.

Rendering

The part of digital animation associated with producing the finished image. Rendering adds aspects of lighting, texture and effects, such as fluidity and atmosphere.

RenderMan

A rendering application developed by Pixar used for digital effects and integrating synthetic effects with live-action footage.

Rostrum camera

A camera mounted on apparatus to allow the filming of artwork or objects with the ability to move the subject or camera incrementally. A basic rostrum has the camera fixed over a target area, while sophisticated rostrum cameras allow movement in three dimensions and control over zoom, focus and aperture.

Rotoscope

The device invented by Max Fleischer, which allowed pre-filmed movement to be traced. Consisting of a projector that could be advanced one frame at a time, action could be displayed from below the frosted glass surface of a drawing board or animation disc, allowing the animator to use it as direct reference.

Simulator

A virtual environment or mechanism that mimics actuality. Simulators were originally designed for training purposes, but have provided the basis for computer games.

Software

The code or non-physical component of digital tools.

Stop-frame technique

Animation made by filming objects one frame at a time. Incremental changes of subject or camera between sequential shots resulting in an illusion of movement.

Track and dolly

The use of a wheeled platform on rails as a position for filming, allowing the camera to move through a scene or, follow action.

Vector games

Part of the first generation of video games that used vector scopes for display rather than TV-like, raster-based cathode ray tubes. *Asteroids* and *Battlezone* are the best known examples.

Virtual world

An environment that does not physically exist, but is made by computer software to appear similar to the real world.

Wireframe

The basic visual representation of a digital object, in a digital version of a sketch. Boundary lines describe the volume of a virtual object.

Zoetrope

A nineteenth-century optical toy consisting of a cylinder with a series of pictures on the inner surface that, when viewed through slits with the cylinder rotating, give an impression of continuous motion.

1930s

1933   Palliard introduces the Bolex H-16 16mm film camera, bringing animation technology closer to the masses.

1950s

1956   The first broadcast-quality video tape recorder (AMPEX VR1000) is developed.

1957   The first computer-scanned image makes an appearance at the National Bureau of Standards, USA.

1958   The first integrated circuit is built by Jack St Clair Kilby at Texas Instruments, USA.

1959   Wesley Clark's construction of the TX-2 computer at MIT includes a cathode ray tube (CRT) screen and is the foundation for critical computer graphics development, including work by Ivan Sutherland.

1960s

1960   Digital Equipment Corporation release the DEC PDP-1, the first graphical, interactive computer.

1961   John Whitney Sr screens *Catalog* – a series of abstract colour animations produced using a motion-controlled rostrum camera.

1962   *Spacewar*, the first computer game, is launched.

1963   Sketchpad, the first computer graphic pen, is invented.

1964   Boeing uses a CG human figure to design airliner cockpit ergonomics.

1965   The first computer art exhibition is held at Technische Hochschule Stuttgart, Germany.

1966   The Mathematical Applications Group, Inc (MAGI) is founded.

1967   The First British CG film (*Modern Mathematics*) is exhibited on IMAX.

1968   Douglas Trumbull designs the slit-scan movie camera for *2001: A Space Odyssey*.

1969   The Special Interest Group for Computer Graphics (SIGGRAPH) is founded.

1970s

1970 Pierre Bézier creates the curve drawing technique for automotive design at Renault.

1971 Gouraud shading is invented at the University of Utah by Henri Gouraud.

1972 Atari is founded by Nolan Bushnell. The video game *PONG* is launched.

1973 CGI in *Westworld* becomes the first mainstream film to use 2D CGI.

1974 Gordon Moore expounds Moore's Law. SIGGRAPH holds its first conference.

1975 Industrial Light & Magic (ILM) is founded by George Lucas to facilitate special effects requirements in the movie *Star Wars*.

1976 *Futureworld* becomes the first mainstream film to use 3D CGI.

1977 Apple II uses the first colour graphic on a personal computer.

1978 Toshihiro Nishikado creates the video game *Space Invaders* for Taito.

1979 Pixar is founded by Edwin Catmull and Alvy Ray Smith III.

1980s

1980 Pacific Data Images (PDI) is founded, creating benchmark software for broadcast digital animation, and eventually joins forces with DreamWorks SKG to produce digital features.

1981 Quantel launches Paintbox – a computer graphic tool for broadcast television.

1982 The first CGI character in mainstream film is realised in *Tron.*

1983 Don Bluth animates the game graphics for Laser Disc-based arcade game *Dragon's Lair*. The Sun-1 Workstation is released by Sun Microsystems.

1984 CGI is used more extensively than ever before in the feature film *The Last Starfighter*. Apple launches the Macintosh.

1985 The first digitally walking character appears in the mainstream feature, *Young Sherlock Holmes*.

1986 Apple acquires Pixar – joining a specialist digital animation facility with a computer company. John Lasseter screens *Luxo Jr* – one of the first digitally animated shorts.

1987 Red's Dream screens Pixar's first digital short to include a human-featured animated character – Lumpy the Clown.

1988 *Tin Toy* becomes the first digitally animated short film to win an Oscar.

1989 The first photorealistic CG creature in cinema is featured in *The Abyss*.

Glossary > **A timeline of digital animation** > Conclusion

1990s

1990 NewTek develop the Video Toaster. Adobe PhotoShop v 1.0 is launched.

1991 The first human CGI appears in the feature film, *Terminator 2: Judgment Day*. 3D CGI appears for the first time in the Disney feature film, *Beauty and the Beast*. The World Wide Web is founded.

1992 The film *Death Becomes Her* makes use of digital animation for visual effects, CAD systems to produce miniature sets, and digital camera controls to govern exposure profiles for slow-motion effects.

1993 The Academy of Motion Picture Arts awards RenderMan a Scientific and Engineering Achievement Award in recognition for the contribution made in integrating digital visual effects with live action, used significantly in 1993 for *Jurassic Park*. *Babylon 5* uses the low-budget, combined video effects system Video Toaster to produce high quality digital effects and animation for a broadcast series.

1994 *ReBoot* becomes the first CGI television series. *Marathon* is released for the Mac.

1995 *Toy Story* becomes the first CGI feature film. DVD reaches the market.

1996 The film *Dragonheart* includes a digital main character in the shape of Draco. *Forrest Gump* makes extensive use of digital effects, including removing Gary Sinise's legs, inserting Tom Hanks into archive footage, and following the path of a feather in the wind.

1997 The film *Spawn* uses computer-simulated textile models to animate the lead character's cape – a major feature in the original comic book. *Men in Black* successfully integrates digital animation and visual effects with physical props and animatronics to produce seamless compositions with live action.

1998 The film *A Bug's Life* becomes the second digital feature from the partnership between Disney and Pixar, and produces a significant contrast in style to *Antz*, which was released in the same year by DreamWorks in partnership with PDI.

1999 The film *What Dreams May Come* becomes indicative of the confidence invested in computer-generated visual effects. It has the majority of its action set in a digital depiction of heaven and hell, which appear concurrently fantastic and photorealistic. George Lucas's *Star Wars Episode I: The Phantom Menace* sees ILM produce the first digitally animated lead character in the shape of Jar Jar Binks.

2000

2000 The success of digitally animated features and a subsequent revival in animation becomes a driving factor in the formation of DreamWorks' Animation Division, signifying an increasing confidence from the mainstream film industry in digital animation.

2001 The first CGI photorealistic characters appear in the feature film *Final Fantasy*. A new Oscar is given for Best Animated Feature Film (*Shrek*). Microsoft releases the Xbox. *The Lord of the Rings: The Fellowship of the Ring* not only produces significant achievements in visual effects on screen, but represents a geographical shift of power from the concentration of Hollywood-centric mainstream effects facilities.

2002 The release of iStopMotion 1.0 software enables Mac users to make stop-frame animation with ease using a digital camcorder.

2003 *The Lord of the Rings: The Two Towers* presents audiences with a convincing, photorealistic, digitally animated lead character in the shape of Gollum.

2004 DreamWorks SKG and PDI spin out DreamWorks Animation establishing a production company charged specifically with making animated features. *Ryan* – a study of a traditional animator's life – wins the Oscar for Best Animated Short. The film *Shark Tale* displays the industry impact of digital animation, drawing a cast including Robert DeNiro, Angelina Jolie, Martin Scorsese and Will Smith. *The Polar Express* embodies the adopted phenomenon from robotics of the Uncanny Valley; as simulated humans are so accurately captured and resolved, emotions of disquiet and unease are provoked in audiences.

2005 *Star Wars Episode III: Revenge of the Sith* becomes the first mainstream feature shot without using film – direct to digital format and entirely within a studio using digitally composited environments in post-production. *Sin City* exploits digital tools to incorporate aesthetics from the film's graphic novel source.

2006 Disney's acquisition of Pixar denotes the full acceptance of digital animation by the established home of mainstream animated features.

Glossary > A timeline of digital animation > Conclusion

Conclusion

The comparatively short history of digital animation has seen the rapid transfer of technology that was the exclusive preserve of industrial and academic research facilities into the domain of creative practitioners and domestic users. Imaging tools developed for engineering, military and scientific purposes have been adopted and adapted for animation, film-making, gaming and a variety of purposes spawning new disciplines and industries, which then add to the aesthetic language of all moving images.

The impact of digital tools has fundamentally changed the processes of production of media, evolving from a peripheral position of support, to becoming part of the core practice of animation and commercial moving-image creation – from pre-visualisation to creation, distribution and broadcast.

Facilitated by the proliferation of the personal computer and associated technologies, such as the Internet and a digitisation of all media types, digital animation is now part of the domestic environment. From YouTube to the animated interfaces of consumer electronics, digital animation has broken out of the traditional domains of cinema and television and become a familiar, even unnoticed, component of the visual landscape.

For the animator, there are gains and losses. It has never been easier to create and show animated movies. The tools of production and exhibition are ubiquitous and require minimal training, and the difference in quality between domestic equipment and professional tools is decreasing with each new generation of technology.

However, these obvious gains must be tempered with the fact that traditional skills and techniques are bypassed through a loss of studios and established training routes in the industry, with cost-conscious producers and commissioners considering the advantages of productions made with 'default' animation and effects. Hope must be taken from the fact that audiences quickly absorb novelty – rapidly assimilating the new, looking beyond mere aesthetics, and demanding greater qualities than mere effect.

Digital animation has also catalysed an interest in animation generally – from an audience point of view, as well as for new practitioners. The technology is now available to both audience and creator, raising expectations and reinforcing the developmental impetus of industrial practice. Simplification of the tools has allowed their use by the widest number of users, not only animators of any discipline and associated practitioners, but interested parties from diverse art and design areas. This provides the opportunity for a reintroduction of animation techniques developed since the origins of moving images, and an addition of new influences from previously disparate practices.

Mark Craste of Studio AKA sums it all up succinctly:

'The wonderful thing about working in CG at this time is that you have all these immensely talented people blazing trails in so many areas, sorting out stuff like water and fire and hair and skin and crowds. And regardless of how interesting those efforts may be creatively, there is a trickle-down effect that enables a lot of us to follow shortly after in their wake, picking up all the new tools, which in the interim have been made idiot-friendly and (relatively) cheap. This information becomes useable by people who, because the tools are now inexpensive, can possibly take greater risks and pursue more adventurous creative paths.'

▼

title
JoJo in the Stars

animator
Marc Craste

The rapid development of digital tools and techniques has provided a renaissance in the medium and increased the pace of evolution. This has resulted in a wider range of style and occurrence in all forms of animation, and a subsequent rise in expectation from the audience.

A timeline of digital animation > **Conclusion** > References and bibliography

Agel, J (1970)
The Making of Kubrick's 2001
New York: Signet

Champlin, C, Spielberg, S, et al. (1992)
George Lucas: The Creative Impulse –
Lucasfilm's First Twenty Years
London: Virgin Books

Elsaesser, T and Barker, A, Eds. (1990)
Early Cinema: Space, Frame, Narrative
London: BFI Publishing

Espemson, J, Ed. (2005)
Finding Serenity: Anti-heroes, Lost Shepherds
and Space Hookers In Joss Whedon's Firefly
Dallas: BenBella Books

Faber, L and Walters, H (2004)
Animation Unlimited:
Innovative Short Films Since 1940
London: Laurence King Publishing

Gomery, D (1991)
Movie History: A Survey
London: Wadsworth Publishing Company

Hanson, M (2004)
The End of Celluloid:
Film Futures in the Digital Age
Hove: RotoVision

Hellemans, A and Bunch, B (1998)
The Timetables of Science:
A Chronology of the Most Important People
and Events in the History of Science
New York: Simon and Schuster

Hertzfeld, A (2004)
Revolution in The Valley:
The Insanely Great Story of
How the Mac Was Made
Cambridge: O'Reilly

Kerlow, IV (2003)
Art of 3D: Computer Animation and Effects
Hoboken: John Wiley & Sons Inc

Levy, S (2000)
Insanely Great: The Life and Times of Macintosh,
the Computer That Changed Everything
New York: Penguin

Maeda, J (2000)
Maeda @ Media
London: Thames & Hudson Ltd

Maestri, G (1999)
Digital Character Animation Book 2:
Essential Techniques Volume 1
Berkeley: New Riders Publishing

Malkiewicz, K (1989)
Cinematography
Columbus: Columbus Books Ltd

McKernan, B (2004)
Digital Cinema: The Revolution in Cinematography,
Post Production and Distribution
Columbus: McGraw-Hill Education

Muybridge, E (2000)
The Human Figure in Motion
New York: Dover Publications Inc

Pierson, M (2002)
Special Effects: Still In Search of Wonder
New York: Columbia University Press

Salt, B (1983)
Film Style and Technology: History and Analysis
London: Starword

Sammon, PM (1997)
Future Noir: The Making of Blade Runner
London: Orion

Sansweet, SJ (1992)
Star Wars: From Concept to Screen to Collectible
San Francisco: Chronicle Books

Smith, TG and Lucas, G (1986)
Industrial Light & Magic: The Art of Special Effects
London: Virgin Books

Stamp, R, Ed. (2005)
The Making of The Hitchhiker's Guide
to the Galaxy:
The Filming of the Douglas Adams Classic
London: Boxtree Ltd

Thomas, F and Johnston, O (1997)
The Illusion of Life: Disney Animation
New York: Hyperion

Titleman, C, Ed. (1979)
The Art of Star Wars
New York: Ballantine Books

Trautman, ES (2004)
The Art of Halo: Creating a Virtual Masterpiece
New York: Ballantine Books

Usai, PC and Scorsese, M (2001)
*The Death of Cinema: History, Cultural Memory
and the Digital Dark Age*
London: BFI Publishing

Vaz, MC (1996)
Industrial Light & Magic: Into the Digital Realm
New York: Del Rey

Wells, P (2005)
The Fundamentals of Animation
Lausanne: AVA Publishing

Whedon, J (2005)
Serenity: The Official Visual Companion
New York: Titan Books Ltd

White, T (1986)
The Animator's Workbook
London: Phaidon

Willis, H (2005)
New Digital Cinema Reinventing the Moving Image
London: Wallflower Press

Withrow, S (2003)
Art: The Graphic Art of Digital Cartooning
Lewes: Ilex

Wozniak, S and Smith, G (2006)
*iWoz: Computer Geek to Cult Icon:
Getting to the Core of Apple's Inventor*
New York: WW Norton & Co Ltd

Wyver, J (1989)
*The Moving Image: International History of Film,
Television and Video*
Oxford: Blackwell Publishers

Filmography

Méliès, G (1902)
Le Voyage dans la Lune

Porter, ES (1906)
Dream of a Rarebit Fiend

Menzies, WC (1936)
The Shape of Things to Come

Hitchcock, A (1958)
Vertigo

Kubrick, S (1968)
2001: A Space Odyssey

Heffron, RT (1968)
Futureworld

Crichton, M (1973)
Westworld

Lucas, G (1977)
Star Wars: A New Hope

Halas, J (1979)
Autobahn

Scott, R (1979)
Alien

Bell, AJW (1981)
*The Hitchhiker's Guide to the Galaxy
(BBC TV series)*

Spielberg, S (1981)
Raiders of the Lost Ark

Lisberger, S (1982)
Tron

Scott, R (1982)
Blade Runner

Jankel, A (1985)
Max Headroom

Levinson, B (1985)
Young Sherlock Holmes

Lasseter, J (1986)
Luxo Jr.

Cameron, J (1989)
The Abyss

Trousdale, G (1991)
Beauty and the Beast

Cameron, J (1991)
Terminator 2: Judgment Day

Zemeckis, R (1992)
Death Becomes Her

O'Bannon, RS (1993)
SeaQuest DSV

Spielberg, S (1993)
Jurassic Park

Straczynski, JM (1994)
Babylon 5

Blair, G, Grace, J, et al. (1994)
ReBoot

Lasseter, J (1995)
Toy Story

Wachowski, A and Wachowski, L (1999)
The Matrix

Lucas, G (1999)
Star Wars: Episode I – The Phantom Menace

Adamson, A (2001)
Shrek

Sakaguchi, H (2001)
Final Fantasy: The Spirits Within

Macomber, D and Thomas, M (2001)
Duality

Hardstaff, J (2001)
Future of Gaming

Whedon, J, Gillum, V, et al. (2002)
Firefly

Howell, G (2003)
How it was that we got to be Angels

Cantolla, D and Garcia, G (2005)
Pocoyo

Jennings, G (2005)
The Hitchhiker's Guide to the Galaxy

McKean, D (2005)
MirrorMask

Whedon, J (2005)
Serenity

Bill, T (2006)
Flyboys

Volkman, C (2006)
Renaissance

Webography

www.alandal.co.uk
The website of contemporary UK-based artists working with digital video technology.

www.mag.awn.com
A comprehensive source of information for all forms of animation.

www.boinx.com
The website of the writers of the iStopMotion animation software.

www.bfi.org.uk
UK-based organisation promoting the understanding and appreciation of Britain's rich film and television heritage and culture.

www.accad.osu.edu/~waynec/history/tree/ overall-list.html
A selection of links to historical events from the timeline of computer graphic imaging.

www.cinesite.co.uk
A post-production company supplying visual effects to the film industry.

www.dam.org
A repository of information and selection of fine artists working with digital imaging technology.

www.digitaltutors.com
Internet-based company offering training resources for digital design and animation.

www.donbluth.com
Don Bluth's home site – a source of information on his classical animation academy.

www.dneg.com
Visual effects company working on providing solutions for feature film and television.

www.cc.gatech.edu/classes/cs6751_97_fall/ projects/abowd_team/ivan/ivan.html
Provides the biography of one of the founding fathers of computer imaging technology.

www.computerarts.co.uk/in_depth/features/ the_history_of_photoshop
An account of the creation of Adobe Photoshop by Thomas and John Knoll.

www.imdb.com
The extensive information archive of film and television production containing cast, crew, statistical and descriptive information.

www.maedastudio.com
John Maeda's own selection of computer graphic artwork covering over a decade of practice and exploring digital media.

www.siggraph.org/artdesign/ profile/whitney/whitney.html
A biography of pioneer digital artist and animator, John Whitney Sr.

www.folklore.org
An anecdotal history of the creation of Apple's Macintosh computers.

www.museum.tv/archives/etv/M/htmlM/ maxheadroom/maxheadroom.htm
A review of the 1987 television series *Max Headroom*, which merged digital imagery with mock digital animation.

www-ee.stanford.edu/~hellman/ opinion/moore.html
Provides an explanation and contextual history of Moore's Law by Professor Martin E. Hellman, Stanford University.

www.kingston.gov.uk/museum/muybridge
The official home of the Muybridge archive at Kingston Upon Thames.

www.spacecentre.co.uk
The UK National Space Centre website – home of the Space Theatre, 360° cinema dome.

www.onedotzero.com
Pan-media production company working with digital technology in fields from education, publishing to film production.

www.tate.org.uk/tateetc/ issue7/fischinger.htm
A concise introduction to the work of Oskar Fischinger – experimental animator and film maker.

www.inwap.com/mf/reboot/ Production.html
An archive of background information on the original creators of the first digitally animated TV series: *ReBoot*.

**www.history.sandiego.edu/gen/
recording/notes.html**
The University of San Diego's history of media
recording technology.

**www.vicon.com/company/
releases/050806.htm**
Home site of one of the industry leaders in motion
capture technology.

www.rodlord.com
Animator Rod Lord's website, including imagery
from the original *The Hitchhiker's Guide to the
Galaxy* TV series.

www.cgsociety.org
Information, folios and links for and by digital
artists of all disciplines.

www.studioaka.co.uk
Animation studio producing independent short
films and sequences for corporate commissions.

www.computerhistory.org
Archives of information and artefacts from the
earliest days of computer history.

**www.microsoft.com/windows/
WinHistoryDesktop.mspx**
Provides a summary of the lifespan of the world's
most popular computer operating system.

**www.stanford.edu/dept/HPS/TimLenoir/
MilitaryEntertainmentComplex.htm**
An extensive academic study of the relationship
between computer simulation and the
military application.

www.theskylounge.net
Homepage of the animation company using digital
tools with traditional sensibilities and skills.

www.willieworld.com
Creator of performance environments and
installations using a range of visual media and
digital technologies.

Digital Animation

As well as gratefully acknowledging the many generous contributors to this book, I would like to express my personal thanks to those who helped behind the scenes in the production of the book including:

Ben Dolman, Gareth Howell and Paul Wells, for coaching and moral support.

Everyone at AVA Publishing especially Brian Morris, Publisher; Renee Last for patience and professionalism; Sanaz Nazemi for picture research and Lucy Tipton for proofreading.

Tamasin Cole for book design.

Ricard Gras and Vanessa Hunt for translation services.

Alex Lucas for an individual eye.

Aisling O'Brien and Helen Arnold for tenacity and humanity.

Ed and Julia Chester for therapy and respite.

Donna Chong for proofreading and tea supply.

John Grace – my constant mentor.

May the Force be with you all.

P3, 138–141 Animation by Onedotzero Industries © Willie Williams 2006; Show Designer / Video Director: Willie Williams, Architect: Mark Fisher, Lighting Director: Bruce Ramus, Video Content: Balarinji Design Studio, Damian Hale, Luke Halls, Ed Holdsworth, Julian Opie, Tony Oursler, Catherine Owens, United Visual Artists, Willie Williams, Run Wrake, Tour Video Director: Stefaan Desmedt, Content Production and Systems Management: Sam Pattinson, Onedotzero Industries

P4, 28 Courtesy of the Kobal Collection / The Art Archive

P4, 48–49 The Kobal Collection / Ladd Company / Warner Bros

P4, 74–75 © William Latham 1992. Produced at IBM UK Scientific Centre / www.williamlatham1.com

P4, 92–93 Courtesy of Rainmaker Entertainment Inc

P4, 136–137 Courtesy of Dr Steven Walker, Lesser General Public Licence (LGPL), Project JMOL

P4, 8–9, 148–149 courtesy of Ricard Gras and LA INTERACTIVA

P7 The Painter © 2003 Hewlett-Packard Development Company LP / 422 South / www.422south.com

P10 Digitised by Andrew Chong

P14 Digitised by Andrew Chong

P16–17 Digitised by Andrew Chong

P19 Courtesy of The Kobal Collection

P20 Digitised by Andrew Chong

P22 Courtesy of Paramount / The Kobal Collection

P25 © Disney Enterprises Inc

P26 © El Friede Fischinger Trust, courtesy of Centre for Visual Music

P30, 37 Courtesy of MGM / The Kobal Collection

P33 Courtesy of Paramount / The Kobal Collection

P34 © The Halas & Batchelor Collection Limited

P38 Photographed by Andrew Chong

P39 Illustration by Andrew Chong

P40–41 Illustration by Andrew Chong

P42 Courtesy of MGM / The Kobal Collection

P43 Courtesy of MGM / UA / The Kobal Collection

P45 Courtesy of Professor Bryan Wyvil

P47 The Kobal Collection / LucasFilm / 20th Century Fox

P50–51 Courtesy of Rod Lord / www.rodlord.com

P52, 58–61 Courtesy of Gary Goldman and Bluth Group Ltd

P55 Photographed by Andrew Chong

P56–57 Courtesy of Walt Disney Pictures / The Kobal Collection

P62–63 Courtesy of Lorimar/Universal / The Kobal Collection

P65 © Chrysalis 1987 / Courtesy of Rod Lord / www.rodlord.com

P66 Courtesy of Dave Hogan / Getty images

P69 Courtesy of New Line Cinema / The Kobal Collection

P69 Courtesy of New Line Cinema / The Kobal Collection

P71 Original Macintosh icons designed by Susan Kare / Illustrations by Andrew Chong

P72–73 Illustration by Andrew Chong

P76–77 Illustration by Andrew Chong

P78, 83 Courtesy of Eidos Interactive Limited

P81 Courtesy of Gareth Howell

P84–87 © Disney Enterprises Inc

P88–89 Courtesy of Studio Ghibli / The Kobal Collection

P90–91 Courtesy of Warner Bros TV / The Kobal Collection

P95 © Disney Enterprises Inc

P96 Courtesy of Rudy Rucker / www.rudyrucker.com

P98–99 Courtesy of Amblin / Universal / The Kobal Collection

P100 Illustration by Andrew Chong

P101 Courtesy of Warner Bros / The Kobal Collection

P102–103 Courtesy of Lucasfilm / The Kobal Collection / Hamshere, Keith

P104, 132–133 Courtesy of Destination / Jim Henson Productions / Goldwyn / The Kobal Collection

P107 Photographed by Andrew Chong

P108–109 Courtesy of Mark Thomas © Crew of Two 2001

P110 Courtesy of Dreamworks LLC / The Kobal Collection

P111 Courtesy of Chris Lee Productions / Square Co / The Kobal Collection

P112–113 Courtesy of © Hardstaff 2001 / www.johnny.hardstaff.com

P114–117 © Christin Bolewski 2006

P119 Courtesy of www.americasarmy.com

P120–121 Courtesy of www.cartoonnetwork.co.uk

P122–123 Pocoyo TM © 2005 Zinkia Entertainment S.L.

P124–125 © 2006 Onyx Films

P127 © Touchstone Pictures 2005, Courtesy of Cinesite

P128–129 Courtesy of Universal Studios / The Kobal Collection

P130–131 Courtesy of Double Negative © 2006 Flyboys Films Ltd

P134–135 Courtesy of Kate Pullinger © the BradField Company Ltd

P142–145 Courtesy of National Space Centre © National Space Centre 2005

P146, 150–151 Courtesy of Rooster Teeth © Rooster Teeth Productions / www.roosterteeth.com; based on Halo © 1985-2001 Microsoft Corporation. All rights reserved.

P152–153, 169 © Studio AKA 2003 / www.studioaka.co.uk

P 154–155 © Dan Lane, SkyLounge 2005 / www.theskylounge.net

P156–157 © Al and Al 2006 / www.alandal.co.uk

P158–159 © Michael Shaw / www.michaelshaw.org

Digital Animation